Influencing
ᴧᴧDeathᴧᴧᴧᴧᴧᴧᴧᴧᴧᴧ

Influencing Death

REFRAMING DYING FOR BETTER LIVING

Penny Hawkins Smith, RN

@HospiceNursePenny

GFB

Published by GFB™, Seattle
www.girlfridayproductions.com

Produced by Girl Friday Productions

Design: Paul Barrett
Production editorial: Reshma Kooner
Project management: Sara Spees Addicott

ISBN (hardcover): 978-1-964721-24-8
ISBN (paperback): 978-1-959411-96-3
ISBN (ebook): 978-1-959411-97-0

Library of Congress Control Number: 2024919035

First edition

*To Mom, for all the heartache I caused
you as I navigated my younger years.
You once told me I had a book in me.
Turns out you were right.*

*There was a time in my life when I wanted
    to die.*
*There was a time in my life when I was
    afraid of dying.*
*There was a time in my life when I made a
    career of caring for the dying.*
*And then there was the time I took to
    social media,*
*started a crusade to normalize death and
    dying,*
and became TikTok famous.

CONTENTS

AUTHOR'S NOTE

I am a hospice nurse. When I tell people I am a hospice nurse, I'm usually met with one of two responses: "That must be so sad" or "You're an angel!" It's not and I'm not. You might be surprised to know that I don't think of hospice nursing as sad; I actually think it's fun. I have met so many fascinating people during what is arguably one of the most intimate times any of us—all of us—will experience in our life: the end of it. I have cried with them, laughed with them, shared stories with them, and cared for them right up until they took their last breath.

Being present with the dying and those they love has brought me joy, happiness, meaning, and purpose.

I am a hospice nurse, but I am not an angel just because of my chosen profession. Being a hospice nurse is what I do; it isn't who I am. Who I am is a human who had a rough start in life and managed to turn my life around. I made a lot of mistakes and I hurt a lot of people. I was a victim and I victimized others. But working with the dying and discovering that I have the compassion, empathy, and resilience to care for them helped me to believe that my mistakes don't define me. That doing bad things did not make me a bad person.

Being present with the dying and those they love has brought me forgiveness—forgiveness for the people who hurt me and, more importantly, forgiveness for myself.

I am a hospice nurse. I have wisdom, knowledge, and stories to share that hopefully will inspire you, influence you, to reframe your thoughts about death and dying. Because when the time comes for a life to end, by honoring the journey and allowing the person to die with comfort and dignity we can view death as a sacred part of life rather than its regrettable, terrible opposite. But as much as this book is about death, it is also about life—my life. I firmly believe that having been a burden to society and then doing what I needed to for a more meaningful existence, I owe it to . . . the universe, if you will, to transparently share my experiences and life lessons so that others might avoid making the same kinds of mistakes I did. Or so, if you have already have, you will also understand that those mistakes don't define you.

Being present with the dying and those they love has brought me peace about life and about death. I hope my stories will bring that to you too.

Now for the disclaimer. The events described in this book are based on my memory of real situations. However, the names and identifying details, such as ages and genders, of all patients and their families discussed in this book have been changed. In addition, each patient's medical history and diagnosis have been changed except where symptoms or disease are integral to the story. With a few exceptions, the names of all colleagues and friends have also been changed. A couple of my friends and all my family members' names have not been changed because they would be pissed if I wrote a whole book and didn't give them a shout-out. Otherwise, any resemblance to persons living or dead resulting from changes to names or identifying details is entirely coincidental and unintentional.

This book does include topics like bullying, addiction, assault, suicide, and obviously death. Although I feel it's important to provide a content warning for most of those things, when it comes to death, a natural part of life, my feeling about a content warning is that it defeats the purpose of the discussion. How are we to normalize talking about it if we have to put a warning label on the conversation? That being said, this book does cover the topic of death and dying. After all, I am a hospice nurse.

PROLOGUE

"When a person is dying. . . ." I began.

I gazed into the image on my iPhone screen and pressed Stop. *Is my hair all right?* I had been wanting a new look and had dyed a section of it bright fuchsia. *Why not?* I'd thought. Bright artificial hair colors were back in style, and reminiscing by adopting the fashion from my youth in the eighties gave me joy. This look would become my social media signature, adored by people my age who wished they had the nerve and young people who thought I was cool. It was also hated by others, who openly asked in my comment section how I could be a professional nurse with a pink streak in my hair.

My iPhone was on the microwave cart in front of me, propped against a book. I had only made a few videos, or TikToks, as they were referred to on the social media app I had recently discovered, so I didn't yet have a tripod. I wore a red T-shirt and just a little makeup. One thing I had quickly learned, even in my TikTok naivete, was that there were lots of filters I could use in lieu of makeup to minimize the lines on my old face. I would have no more than one minute to tell my story, as that was the maximum amount of time allowed by TikTok back then. I wasn't like your typical social media influencers—pretty young women peddling makeup, seasoned chefs creating fancy dishes, or nubile twentysomethings doing trendy dances. I was a fifty-seven-year-old hospice nurse, and I was about to tell a story about a dying woman.

Like many people, I discovered TikTok during the shutdown due to the COVID-19 pandemic in 2020. One night when I was watching television, I saw a story about a pediatrician who had been using the social media platform to educate on the importance of vaccinating children who was receiving death threats as a result. I quickly downloaded the app and searched for the doctor. It didn't take me long before I was sucked into a rabbit hole of videos that ranged in content from people doing short little skits to lip-synching lines to movies to dancing. Specifically, shuffle dancing. And there were tutorials!

My husband worked nights, leaving me alone in the house. No longer able to go to the YMCA to work out, I decided that learning how to do this shuffle dancing would be a fun way to get my exercise in. After all, I loved to dance, so how hard could it be? It was harder than I thought, and—plot twist—I never did learn how to do it. But, having been a bit of a performance geek earlier in my life, I soon jumped on other TikTok trends and made a few videos that got barely any views. I wasn't surprised. As much as I hate the term and don't feel like I fit into the category, I am a boomer, and my generation wasn't necessarily welcome on the popular app. So one day I decided to go in a different direction and talk about what I know best.

As a certified hospice and palliative care nurse, I am passionate about educating about the end-of-life. Not surprisingly, people get scared and worried when they see things happening to their dying person they haven't ever seen before. Throughout my career working as a hospice nurse, I have discovered that one of the best ways to ease the worries of the families of dying people is to normalize death. That is to say, to explain all the normal but unusual things that can happen to a person who is dying. Things such as terminal secretions. More commonly known as the death rattle, this gurgling sound is just a noise resulting from a buildup of saliva the dying person is no longer able to swallow. I also reassure them that the changes they are observing in their dying loved one—changes in breathing, mouth agape, eyes in a fixed stare—are, again, normal.

"She keeps having long pauses in breathing," they tell me fretfully.

"That's normal," I say.

"It is?"

"Yes."

(Huge sighs of relief.)

But now, I wasn't at the bedside of a dying patient; I was on a social media app about to go viral by broaching the number-one subject everyone seems to want to avoid: death.

It's do or die, I thought, pun intended, and pressed Record again.

> *When a person is dying a natural death, there are a few signs that will tell you the end is near. When I was a new hospice nurse working in a care center, we had a patient whose daughter was a nun. So she had a lot of visitors who were nuns.*
>
> *One evening, the last nun was visiting, and she came to the nurses' station and said to me, "She's gone."*
>
> *I said, "Oh," and stood up and grabbed my stethoscope.*
>
> *She said, "No, no, no—her body is still here doing the work of dying, but her spirit has left. You can see it in her eyes."*
>
> *Well, being a new hospice nurse, I was really curious, so I went into the room to look at the patient. Sure enough, she had this glazed-over,*

faraway look. I now know that many hospice nurses call that looking at heaven or the God stare. And since then, of course, I've seen it hundreds of times.

When they say that the eyes are the window to the soul, I really believe that. Because when the soul leaves, you can see it in their eyes.

I stopped the recording.

Before I became a hospice nurse, I don't think I ever really gave much consideration to what a natural death is. It wasn't that I didn't think about death. The truth is, I suffered from death anxiety, so I thought about it constantly. One might even say obsessively. I worried about death day and night, mostly at night, when I would lie awake, seeking solace from my then-husband. "But what if there's nothing after we die?" I would cry in anguish. To which his unhelpful reply was "Well, it won't matter because you won't know!" This might be why he is my then-husband and not my now-husband.

But back to natural death. Most people would think of natural death in terms of dying from natural causes, but in hospice there's more to it than that. I think to understand what a natural death is by hospice standards, we first have to look at what an unnatural death is. This is best explained through tales told to me by many nurses who came to work in hospice after they grew weary of seeing people dying in a most unnatural way—patients in the intensive care unit (ICU) hooked up to machines, with tubes jammed into every orifice of their bodies. Or on the oncology floor, where patients were injected with lifesaving treatments that promised them a cure or even just a little more time but delivered misery and suffering. Futile attempts at prolonging life instead of allowing a person who's dying to die. Do you see where I'm going with this?

A natural death means you get to die naturally, without a

gazillion things going on to try to keep you alive. It's allowing your body to shut down through a natural and normal dying process that all life on Earth eventually must succumb to, a process that involves specific stages, symptoms, and hallmark signs. The earliest signs are eating less, sleeping more, and socially withdrawing.

After those comes transition, which I think of as turning the corner. I explain it to my patients' families like this, "We who are not sick are more living than we are dying, but when a person has a terminal illness, they get to a point when they are more dying than they are living. That is transition." The transitioning phase usually signifies the last weeks of life. Significant changes start to happen during this time, some of them quite profound. People who are transitioning will sometimes talk about seeing visions of deceased relatives and even pets. These deathbed visions are really misnamed, because they imply that a person is in their actual bed, ready to die at any moment. However, a person can start having these visions weeks before they are bedbound. This isn't something caused by medications or confusion; many people can clearly state who they are seeing. I've walked into more than a few rooms where a person was adamant they were seeing somebody in front of them when no one else was in the room.

People sometimes speak metaphorically about their impending death. Though some dispense with the metaphors, opting for the more straight-shooting "I'm ready to die," I've often heard patients say things like "I need to pack" or "I'm going on a trip."

More than once, the wife or husband of a dying patient has told me they argued with their spouse all night. "He kept telling me he wants to go home, and I told him, 'You are home; this is our house, where you've lived for forty years!'" I explain that sometimes "home" has a different meaning now, which is inevitably followed by a relieved understanding.

Other things that happen during transition can include physical symptoms: mottling (a purple or blue discoloration usually on the hands or feet caused by changes in circulation) and a diminishing ability to swallow food, liquids, medications, and as I previously said, their own spit. Confusion and disorientation are very common. Sometimes it even seems the person is here and then—somewhere else.

The last stage of the dying process is actively or imminently dying. This is the point of no return. People are generally unresponsive, or if they do respond, it's without meaning or purpose. Eyes and mouth are usually open, the skin might look waxy and pale or yellowish, and sometimes the eyes appear to change color too. As with most aspects of life, not everyone experiences the same pathway to death. Some may have a few symptoms, some may have all, and each person's visitation of the stages varies in length. For some, this process could take weeks, and for others, less. Sometimes people skip all of it and just drop dead, although I'm here to tell you that is rare. But this final stage, this actively dying part, is when we know the end is near.

If you're thinking a natural death is like a natural birth, probably because the term "transitioning" is used in both, it's not. A natural birth means the expectant mother labors and births her child without any medications. None. But a natural death allows the dying person to take medications that will ease their suffering. The dying process isn't necessarily always painful; our bodies instinctively know how to stop living. A person with dementia may not experience any pain that requires medications. But someone with a disease like cancer can suffer greatly due to pain or other symptoms caused by the disease and need to have those symptoms managed with drugs. Most often with morphine, a narcotic that is a first-line medication used in hospice.

Although I never worked in the ICU, I didn't need to have

the hindsight of watching people be tormented on their death-beds to understand it was probably not the best way to die; I inherently knew. But unlike my colleagues from the ICU who decided enough was enough and eventually sought out refuge by becoming hospice nurses, working in hospice was a different kind of reprieve for me. One that would, in my mind anyway, absolve me from some of the "sins" of my past. My pathway to success as a hospice nurse began littered with wreckage from poor life decisions fueled by drugs, alcohol, and very bad relationship choices. It took me many years to get my shit together. In fact, my nursing career didn't start until I was forty-two years old!

So, while my nurse friends in acute care went to hospice for patient-driven reasons, my decision was more self-serving. That's not to say I wasn't able to find compassion for my patients. If I'm honest, I think going through the bullshit I endured in my younger years (admittedly much of it my own doing) helped me not only to find compassion for others but build the strength of character needed to face death on the regular. As much as people want to say it's a "calling" and that hospice nurses are "angels," we are a tough crowd with broad shoulders who thrive on dark humor and challenging patients. We think of ourselves as being "MacGyver" nurses for our ability to come up with solutions to perplexing situations, such as wounds the likes of which we've never encountered and certainly didn't learn about in nursing school (cancer can do some unimaginable things to the human body). As far as being an angel, personally, I've always hated being called that. My past is proof there is nothing angelic about me. And as for it being a calling, that sounds so trite. I think of working in hospice as service work, sacred work, and for me, kind of a route to redemption.

Anyway, let me tell you more about the story that inspired that first TikTok. Encountering nuns at the first hospice care center where I worked wasn't that unusual. It was a Catholic-owned facility, and we had nun volunteers who sometimes worked the desk. I had a fascination with nuns that started when I was a child. There was a TV show called *The Flying Nun* that featured a young novice who used her nun hat to fly—I was obsessed. One day I announced to my mom that I wanted to be a nun. "You're not even Catholic," she scolded. I wasn't anything at all; going to church wasn't ever a part of my childhood.

Regardless of having learned that nuns couldn't really fly, I continued to hold them in high esteem. So, when I first started working at the care center, I felt a little awkward around them. Like what if they could sense my shady past? But they were warm and friendly, and I became friends with Sister Catherine, who was only a few years my senior but was so worldly and mature it felt like there was a greater gap in our ages. Sister Catherine and I would chat at lunchtime, and she shared many things about Catholicism and being a nun. One thing I hadn't realized was that a nun didn't have to be a never-married virgin. In fact, another of the nun volunteers had been married and had a child. She went through some ceremony to become pure again, or some such thing, and was then able to commit to her life of servitude to God and the pope.

One of the most interesting things Sister Catherine told me was about the last rites that are administered at the end of life. She said that the practice had mostly been discontinued in favor of the sacrament of the sick ritual. The intent of the last rites was to swoop in at the last second and administer the sin-absolving blessing just before the person died so they didn't have another chance to sin. But if a dying person received the last rites and then didn't die right away, there was a chance they might sin again, meaning they would have to keep getting the ritual. So with the advancement of medical technology and the ability to bring people back from the brink, they needed to change their blessing to last longer. The way Sister Catherine explained it to me, the sacrament of the sick had a more lasting effect and would cover the person in case they sinned after getting the blessing. (When I later retold this story to other members of the faith, I was informed that wasn't quite the way it worked. So, Sister Catherine might have made the story a little more palatable for a non-Catholic like me, but I still think that her version is way more intriguing.)

The care center had twenty rooms total, divided into two wings, east and west. The east wing had fifteen beds, so there were more patients because there were more, albeit smaller, rooms. The west wing had fewer rooms and they were suites, so we tended to keep them in reserve for patients with bigger families or more visitors. Because of this, the west wing was quieter, especially in the evening. As I said, seeing nuns at the care center wasn't that unusual, but seeing a whole slew of them coming and going day after day was a little out of the norm. Most of them were young, and even though they didn't wear the traditional habits, there was a look of conservatism about the way they dressed and reverence in the way they held themselves.

When the nun told me she could see the spirit had left my patient's body, I was more than curious—I was fascinated. Although I am not religious, I consider myself spiritual. Hearing an authority on all things related to spirituality tell me she had observed the spirit leave didn't sound like some smarmy religious-based mumbo jumbo. I could feel in my spirit, my soul—whatever you want to call it—she was telling the truth.

After the nun left, I practically ran into that room. It was dimly lit, and the patient's back was to the door, so I had to walk around the bed to see her face. Her neck was hyperextended as if she wanted to look up at the ceiling, and her jaw was dropped open, showing her well-worn teeth. This is a normal end-of-life sign. She was in her eighties, but her face looked younger than that, probably due to the wrinkles being smoothed out by the neck extension and open mouth. I didn't have to touch her or attempt to rouse her to know she would be completely unresponsive. Her breaths were even and deep, working toward death. Occasionally, her breathing would pause for what seemed like a minute. The moment I looked into this dying woman's eyes, I knew what the nun had meant. Her blue eyes, which I'm sure had once been crystal clear, were hazy, and although she seemed to be staring at the ceiling, it was evident she wasn't seeing anything. I really did have the sense that her soul or spirit had already vacated her dying body.

As I said, I'm not religious, but I don't think one has to be religious to come to that conclusion. Anyway, in the end, it doesn't matter what religion you practice, what deity you worship, or what you believe happens after death. The reality of an afterlife is what it is (or isn't, if it doesn't exist!). Whether there is something in the great beyond or not, we have no control over it from this side. But many believe in the idea of a soul. I think holding on to that last little bit of humanity, the possibility that there is some part of us that leaves our body and will continue on in some way, captivates most people.

What I saw in that dying woman's eyes assured me that we do have another life after this one. I don't know what that looks like or how it works, but I believe the soul goes on. Realizing that gave me a kind of peace around death I had never before experienced. I was hooked on not just caring for dying people but witnessing this beautiful, sacred ending of one journey and the beginning of the next.

It wouldn't be long before I was hooked on something else—making TikToks.

CHAPTER 1

FOR GOD'S SAKE, FORGET THE HARPS!

"The destination is on your right," Siri announced, overriding the Partridge Family song that I had been blasting to distract myself as I pulled my Prius up to a small, gray single-story home. The yard looked like it had been nicely landscaped at one time but hardly experienced any attention recently. The lawn was brown with pops of yellow and green from dandelions gone unchecked. The curtains were drawn shut and, if it hadn't been for the call I had made to the occupant earlier in the day to confirm my arrival, I would have thought the house vacant. I picked up my notepad from the passenger seat, or my "office," as I usually referred to it, and double-checked the address. Satisfied that Siri had delivered me to the right destination, I shut off the car and opened the door, swinging my legs out. I reached into the back seat and pulled out the roller bag holding all the tools of my trade: a stethoscope, laptop, gloves, hand sanitizer, and all the other accouterments a nurse might need to care for a dying patient.

As I proceeded up the walkway, I saw wide eyes peering around the door, which was now cracked slightly open. I waved.

"Hi, I'm Penny, your hospice nurse. Are you Mrs. Woods?"

The woman frantically gestured for me to come in. "Yes, yes, I'm Lorraine Woods—you can call me Lorraine," she said anxiously. "Thank God you're here! Please come in. He's not eating, he's not drinking, and I can only get him to wake up for a few minutes. I don't know what's wrong, and I'm so scared." Lorraine crumpled over, and I could see tears glistening on her cheeks.

The person in question was Brandon, Lorraine's twenty-two-year-old son. He had been admitted to hospice only a day ago. The oncologist had finally made the determination that the chemotherapy, meant to poison his cancer, was likely contributing to the destruction of his young body and not working to slow the rapidly growing tumors.

I followed Lorraine into the home, down a hall, twisting one way and then the next. The house was clean, but as I was accustomed to seeing in homes where the focus was caregiving for a dying patient, there was a fair amount of clutter. We arrived in the living room, where Brandon was spending his last days of life. The lights were dim, and classical music played quietly in the background. *An odd choice*, I thought, *given Brandon's young age.*

Lorraine pointed at a hospital bed in the corner of the room, as if I wouldn't have noticed it otherwise. In the bed lay a young man whose hazel eyes were partially open, though he did not appear to be looking at anything. His sandy blond hair was unkempt, and his gaunt pale face didn't closely resemble what had surely been a handsome young man's before falling victim to his insidious disease. Soft, gurgling noises could be heard with each breath.

I reached out to him, placing my hand on his arm and lightly shaking it. Hospice nursing requires a gentle touch, and a patient's response is never checked with vigorous shaking. If a patient doesn't respond to a quiet presence, I leave them alone. But my touch was enough to rouse my young patient, and he opened his eyes fully, looking up at me.

"Brandon, I'm Penny, your nurse. How are you doing today?"

Brandon stared at me for a moment, took a deep rattling breath, then closed his eyes. I was experienced enough to know that Brandon was probably in his last few days of life and decided to forgo any checking of vital signs. I am a firm believer that the dying process should be minimally interrupted, if at all. I also knew the readings I would get on my nursing equipment would be meaningless if I didn't plan to intervene. The needs of a dying patient are better met by evaluating their comfort based on how they look, not the numbers on a blood pressure cuff. Brandon appeared to be peacefully and painlessly dying.

"Do you think he's suffering?" Lorraine asked quietly. She had been so silent that I almost forgot she was still in the room.

"He looks quite comfortable, actually. His face is very relaxed," I said, running my finger across his smooth forehead slowly. "This is usually very creased when a person is in pain."

The angst Lorraine had shown when I first arrived began to return. "Why is he making that noise? It sounds like he is drowning!"

I did my best to reassure Lorraine the noise was normal. "Brandon just isn't able to swallow anymore, and saliva is building up in his throat," I explained. "When the air moves over it, it makes that rattling noise." Lorraine looked worriedly at Brandon. "Lorraine," I said firmly, trying to get her attention, "it's just a noise, that's all. But we can help a little by changing his position."

I grabbed the bed remote attached to the side rail and lowered the head of the bed down. Then I motioned for Lorraine to walk around to the opposite side of the bed. "Pick up the sheet that's under him, and we're going to slide him up on three," I directed her. She grasped the draw sheet gingerly at first but then gripped it tightly. I leaned over to Brandon and caught his gaze. "We're just going to pull you up in the bed a little."

He closed his eyes briefly in acknowledgment. "One . . . two . . . three," we counted together before sliding him toward the top of the bed. Using the draw sheet, I gently moved Brandon over onto his side, facing his mom, and stuffed a pillow behind his back to prop him up. I picked up the bed remote again and raised the head of the bed. After a few moments, the rattling from Brandon's airway began to slow down and, with a gentle exhalation, the noise stopped.

I took Lorraine's hand and looked directly into her eyes. I knew at times like these it was often best to be very direct. The stress of losing a loved one can often cause people to misunderstand the message. "Do you know about what's going on with Brandon?"

Lorraine's gaze shifted to the floor as she shook her head slowly back and forth. "Not much," she said, then lowered her voice to a barely audible whisper. "The oncologist told me the treatment wasn't working and they thought hospice was the best thing for him."

"What do you know about hospice?" I probed.

Lorraine continued to stare at the floor. "Well, I looked it up on the internet and it said that hospice starts when the doctors think a person has six months to live," she said quietly.

"Six months or *less*," I gently clarified. "Has any doctor told you how long they think Brandon has to live?"

Lorraine began to cry and raised her voice so suddenly it startled me a little. "No! But I think I need to know!"

In hospice, we say that if you want to know how long a patient has left to live, don't ask the doctor, ask the hospice nurse. When a person comes onto hospice, they rarely, if ever, continue to see their regular doctor. One of the selling points for hospice is that people can spend what little time they have left avoiding the ER and doctor visits. So while hospice nurses have eyes on the dying person and see all the telltale signs of approaching death, doctors really don't get that opportunity. The exception is doctors who work in critical care, but by the time it is apparent that death is going to be the outcome in those cases, they've likely missed the earlier signs. Hospice nurses know best. But there is a mitigating factor that has to be considered when anyone is trying to predict death—it's unpredictable. We typically give estimates in time frames, like weeks to months, days to weeks, hours to days, minutes to hours.

Still holding her hand, I walked Lorraine to the corner of the room and guided her to sit on a small sofa. Then I sat down next to her. I took a deep, deliberate breath to ensure the cadence of my speech would be precise and firm without being cold.

"Well, we never really know for sure. I'm going to give you a guess, and it will be the worst-case scenario. That way, if I'm right you're prepared . . . and if I'm wrong, it's a gift." I searched Lorraine's face for a signal of approval to continue the difficult conversation. Lorraine stared back at me intently, nodding her head. "I would say it could be possibly hours to days. He is young, and sometimes young people last a little longer. But that rattling noise usually means things are changing. He looks very close."

Lorraine's eyes welled up with tears. "What do I do? I don't know what to do."

I reached into my bag and pulled out a plastic-wrapped sponge-on-a-stick. "Let's talk about medications, and I'll show you some things you can do to keep him comfortable."

Having given Lorraine a crash course in end-of-life care, including administering morphine and using the sponge to keep his mouth moist, I asked if there was anything else I could do for her or if she had any more questions before I left.

Lorraine drew in a deep breath, as if to compose herself before speaking.

"No. I can do this. I can do this for my baby."

Before leaving, I walked over to Brandon and touched his cheek. I leaned over and whispered to him, "Brandon, if I don't see you again, good journey to you." I let Lorraine know I would be calling tomorrow to check on her but told her not to hesitate to call if she needed anything at all in the meantime.

"Oh, one more thing. Does he like to listen to classical music?" I asked.

Lorraine looked at me, seemingly confused, then stammered, "Uh, I-I guess he probably doesn't really. I-I just thought it seemed like the right thing to be playing." I told her she might think about playing something he would normally listen to. She looked down at Brandon and then back at me, nodding her head. "Okay, thanks."

As I headed to my next patient, the traffic was heavy, as usual, and wanting to distract myself enough to avoid getting irritated, I called my sister, Laura.

"Hello?" Laura answered groggily.

"Biiiiitch?" I sang out. Although our relationship earlier in life had been one of fierce competition, this greeting of endearment had become so common in our family, even our daughters and our seventy-three-year-old mother used it on occasion!

Laura answered back, "Biiiiitch, it's too damn early! What's up?" I told her about my day so far and the youngster I was taking care of, without breaching any privacy, of course. "Oh, wow," Laura replied, nonplussed. Even though I had been sharing my hospice experiences with her for many years, I got the sense she still didn't quite know how to react to my deathbed stories. "Are you going to be able to make it for dinner tonight?" she quickly asked after a moment of awkward silence.

I told her I would need to bail; I just had too much going

on. She suggested lunch tomorrow instead, but I wasn't sure about that either. "I can do it if my caseload gets lighter."

Laura paused thoughtfully before speaking. "You mean if someone dies?"

"Yep. You know things are rough when someone has to die for me to get time off!"

Laura chuckled; she was more comfortable with the dark humor than with the sad tales I told. "Right. So did you call just to use me as your commute bitch?" she asked, acting annoyed.

I laughed. "You know it!"

Laura sighed deeply. "Okay, hanging up now. Let me know about tomorrow."

"I'm almost at my destination, so I'm done with you now, anyway," I said, before hanging up.

Almost immediately after I ended the call with my sister, my phone rang again. A woman's voice was barely audible, but through the crying, I heard, "It's Lorraine. I need you. Something's different with Brandon and I don't know what to do." Although hospice offers 24/7 nursing support by phone, we aren't always able to drop everything and go see patients. But I still had time to spare before my next appointment, and I was close enough to circle back to see what was going on.

People want to know what to do when their person is dying. But there comes a time when caring for the dying person is less about doing and more about being. Just being present. I instructed Lorraine to hold Brandon's hand, and I let her know I was on my way.

I arrived at the house fifteen minutes later. As I walked up the path to the door, I could hear rhythmic bass playing so loudly the windows were rattling. I knocked on the door and yelled for Lorraine, not sure she would even be able to hear me over the driving beat of music. A woman's voice called out from inside, "Come in." Inside, I could hear the words to the music that was blasting from a speaker on the table next to

Brandon's bed, a rap song replete with profanity, "Fuck this . . . fucking fuck . . ." I'm sure there were more words, but those were all that stood out to me.

Lorraine was standing next to Brandon, holding his hand. His breathing had changed again, and he was now gasping like a fish out of water. "Wow, that's a definite change of tempo," I yelled.

Lorraine picked up an iPhone from the nightstand and adjusted the volume down. "You were right. When I put his music on, he just seemed more peaceful. Of course, it makes me want to die to have to listen to it," she said, sort of half laughing, half crying. "I can't believe I'm joking right now; I just want it to be over," she sobbed, turning her gaze to the dying young man. "I want his suffering to end. Is that just awful for me to say?" She looked back at me.

I paused, not saying anything right away, to allow space for silence. Then I reached out and wrapped my arm around Lorraine's back. "Lorraine," I said softly, "look at his face. Look at how peaceful he is." I squeezed her shoulder tenderly as I pulled a tissue out of a box and handed it to her. "But I know this is hard for you."

Lorraine sniffed and looked up at the ceiling, as if to gather her thoughts. "What can I do?"

I walked over to Brandon's side. "Talk to him, tell him you'll be okay."

Lorraine began sobbing again. "But it's not okay!"

"Of course it's not okay," I acknowledged. "It's never okay for someone to lose their loved one, especially their child." I thought for a minute. "Lorraine, tell him what he means to you."

Lorraine inhaled deeply and picked up Brandon's hand, clutching it to her heart. "Brandon, I'll never forget holding your tiny little hand when the doctor first handed you to me. I had been so scared, after your dad died, that I wouldn't be able to take care of you. Then you opened your eyes and looked right into mine, and it was like your dad was speaking to me, through you, and I just knew we would be okay." Lorraine looked up at me.

Now, I will pause here to tell you that I can control my emotions quite well, and I am not one who usually cries in the line of duty. But when something takes hold of my heart, I've been known to shed a tear or two, and that moment definitely touched my heart. I brushed a tear off my cheek and smiled back approvingly.

Lorraine swallowed so hard I could hear it. "Brandon, I'm going to miss you. But I'm going to be okay." Brandon took one last breath, and then there was stillness. Lorraine looked over at me. I placed my stethoscope and listened intently. Nothing. I nodded my head to acknowledge that the young man had indeed died. As Lorraine folded over Brandon and began to sob, I got up and walked toward the kitchen. "I'm just going to sit in there and give you some time," I told her.

I sat down at the dining table and paused for a moment, putting my hands up to my eyes to quell the tears I could feel starting to accumulate. It was a privilege to witness a beautiful death with such impeccable timing, especially since people don't always die just when their loved one says their piece. I shook my head sharply to snap myself out of it, pulled my phone out of my pocket, and dialed my office to report Brandon's death. After a few moments, Lorraine appeared in the doorway. Her cheeks were blotchy from crying, but she looked composed.

"I can't thank you enough. I don't know how you do this every day. You're amazing."

This type of praise always made me a little uncomfortable. "No, no. I'm really not," I told her, picking up my bag and heading for the door. "It was such a privilege and an honor to be here with you, Lorraine. Thank you."

Lorraine walked slowly in front of me, then stopped and turned around to face me. She grabbed my hand and squeezed it. "Say what you want," she told me, "but I think you must be an angel."

I'm not, I thought. *I am very human.* And what I've realized is that the same compassion we hold for others can take a hell of a lot of practice to hold for ourselves.

CHAPTER 2

MY EARLY LIFE IN BULLET POINTS

I can't pinpoint when my life went off the rails. To be honest, it's more like I can't remember due to night after night of a drug- and alcohol-driven existence. I do know I wasn't always a hot mess. The unraveling was a process.

I was born in 1962 on Guam, where my dad, an enlisted Navy mechanic from Texas, had been stationed. When I got a little older and became infatuated with the television show *Gilligan's Island*, I thought it was so cool I was born on a tropical island like the one the seven castaways were marooned on.

"Mom, am I Guamanian?" I asked one day.

"No, of course not!" Mom scoffed. "Just because you were born on Guam doesn't mean you're Guamanian." I was a little confused by her answer. After all, my dad called himself a Texan, and my mom, being from a little town in Manitoba, Canada, claimed to be a Canadian.

My sister, Laura, was born only thirteen months after me. I was too young to remember any of the jealous feelings I had after being robbed of my babyhood by a newborn. My mom tells tales of remorse for letting a neighbor talk her into weaning me off of the bottle before Laura was born, which resulted in me stealing hers every chance I got. I started my life of crime before I was even two years old! We bounced from Guam to California and finally settled for a while in Oak Harbor, Washington, a small military town on Whidbey Island. There, my brother, Brad, was born, and our family was complete.

My home life was pretty much average, I think. My parents took us on family vacations and surprised us with trips to the drive-in movie theater, Disneyland, and even once to a pet store to get Dutchess, a sweet sheltie-mix puppy. My siblings and I were disciplined appropriately when warranted—although I seemed to get punished more than they did (and there might have been a reason for that). Mom and Dad stayed married until my dad's death, so if that is the standard by which to measure a family unit, I guess you could say ours was functional.

My earlier childhood was mostly happy except for the bullies. I can't remember why, but when I started the first grade, I developed a fear of asking my teacher to let me go to the bathroom. This was probably because Mrs. Graves, my teacher, was very mean. It was a long walk home from school, and by the time I got there, I often had to pee so bad I couldn't get into the house in time. I would stand at the door, crying hysterically for my mom to open it, too upset to think about putting my books down and opening it myself. She never seemed to get there fast enough, and I would end up relieving myself right there on the porch. All the while my classmates would stop on the sidewalk, jeering at me. It became such a regularly scheduled event that kids would wait for me to arrive, giggling and pointing as the yellow urine ran down my bare legs.

I should also mention that in those days, the sixties, girls were not allowed to wear pants to school. Can you believe that? We've advanced socially a long way, if for nothing else than to prevent little girls from freezing their legs off in the winter! Anyway, my mom finally recognized the need to talk to my teacher about it, and Mrs. Graves started asking me if I needed to go to the bathroom toward the end of the day. Problem solved and bullying stopped. At least for a few years.

We stayed in Oak Harbor until after I finished the fourth grade, when we moved to San Diego, California. A child's memory being what it is, I had only recalled ever living in Oak Harbor, so moving away from my home and my best friend, Lisa, was torture. I adapted to my new surroundings quickly, though, and made several new friends. Once again, we lived in a military community, off base this time, but still surrounded by other military families. The weather suited me and there were plenty of activities to keep me busy. I played baseball and hide-and-go-seek with the neighbor kids, but mostly my days were filled with roller skating and bike riding with my friend Courtney. This went on through fifth and sixth grade, but Courtney was a year older than I was, and when she started junior high, we spent less and less time together. In the meantime, Violet and her sister, Nicole, came into the picture, and we, along with Laura, started hanging out. But Violet and Nicole were less excited by the things I had been entertaining myself with, and they found a fun and very exciting new activity for us to do: shoplifting.

I couldn't believe how easy it was for us to just walk into a store, pick up a paper bag, load it up, and simply leave. The haul usually included candy, makeup, coloring books, and cigarettes, which we smoked under the streets in the dry storm-drain tunnels. It was an eclectic mix of items that reflected the coming-of-age period in our lives; we were stuck between the kids we'd been and the teenagers we were turning into. We didn't ever hit the stores near our homes. It seemed safer to be in San Ysidro, a little border town. We were proud of our abilities, and at the height of our shoplifting careers, we walked out of a store with a whole roasted chicken! What can I say? We were hungry!

Laura never felt good about the theft, and although she

would accompany us and partake in the booty, she wouldn't participate in the actual deed. One day Mom sent us on an errand to the Alpha Beta, a local grocery store, and I decided I needed to pick up a few extra things. It was the first time I attempted to shoplift without Violet and Nicole. Laura, apparently sensing disaster, tried her best to talk me out of it. After months of experience, I felt like a pro, even without my accomplices there. I confidently walked into the store, picked up a large grocery bag, and proceeded to fill it up with not only the things I wanted but with my mom's shopping list items too. Once satisfied with the bulging bag of goods, I casually walked outside with Laura tailing behind me. Three steps out of the store and I suddenly felt the arms of someone swooping me up off the ground. I screamed, clinging tightly to my bag, and turned my head to see the terrifying face of an old man. I reached out and ran my sharp fingernails down the side of his cheek, leaving a dotted line of red. Meanwhile, Laura screamed frantically at people passing by, "Someone help my sister! *Help my sister!*" Of course, they all knew what neither she nor I did—this man was the store security guard, and I was busted.

The ride home with my dad was, still to date, one of the worst moments of my life. Laura had run all the way home, so it was just me and him in the car. The silence was excruciating. He left the punishment to my mom, although according to her, he did make the recommendation of a butt whipping. She chose instead to ground me to my room. Honestly, a blistered ass would have been preferable over their obvious disappointment in me. As soon as I was allowed outside again, I promptly gave away everything I had ever stolen. I wanted nothing to do with any of it, and I never stole another thing again. After that, I found new friends without illegal hobbies and tried to toe the line as much as possible.

My new pastime became boys, and I soon started hanging

out with Pat, a long-haired, sandy blond punk who had a few bad habits of his own. Thankfully, my family ended up moving back to Oak Harbor before our budding romance went any further than hand-holding after a school dance. I used to say if it wasn't for moving away from SoCal, I would have ended up a criminal. Then, I'd remember that I still did—but at least I was deterred from fucking up for a little while longer.

Going back to Oak Harbor meant being able to resume my friendship with my best friend, Lisa. I was so excited and wanted to tell her right away, but I also wanted to surprise her, so I did not write to let her know the good news. As soon as we arrived, I called her. We had only communicated by mail because of the long-distance charges, so she was a little surprised.

"Guess what? I'm here!" I blurted out.

"Here in Oak Harbor?" she asked. I was a little confused that she didn't sound as excited as I felt. It was a Friday, and I asked her if we could get together. My mom had already told me she would give me a ride.

"Well, I'm going to the movies tonight," she said. There was only one theater in town, and it was close to our new house, so I told her I would be able to meet her there.

Silence.

This is weird, I thought.

Finally, she spoke. "I'm meeting up with Linda and Melanie and, well, I haven't *seen* you yet."

I suddenly realized what the problem was. We hadn't been together for three years, and she was concerned I wouldn't fit in to her new crowd. I remembered that as we'd parted ways, she'd been dragged off by Linda and Melanie, before we could even say a proper goodbye. Even though we were just going into the fifth grade at the time, the clique vibe had been strong. Lisa had felt bad that she'd let them do that, or so she had said in a letter to me, but now here she was prioritizing them over me, again. My feelings were hurt, although she ended the call by saying we would see each other on Monday at school. So, I thought, maybe she *wasn't* worried about being embarrassed by me.

Nope, I had been right the first time. To her credit, she did try to help me by having me over to her house for a sleepover, where she tried to teach me to do my hair and makeup and gave me a few articles of trendy clothes. The popularity lesson ended with her telling me I wouldn't be able to be friends with Diana and Marnie, two new friends I had made. "They aren't in the popular group, so you can't really hang out with them if you want to be popular," she said in a serious tone. I agreed to her condition, though secretly I knew I would not end these new friendships. It made no sense to me to try to gain popularity by excommunicating people!

So my relationship with Lisa went by the wayside, and Diana, Marnie, and I started our own clique. Nevertheless, this was the eighth grade, and we were teenage girls. If I knew then what I know now—that teenage girls are bitches—I might have better memories of those formative years. Unfortunately, that is not how things went.

Diana got me involved in dog 4-H, a club for teens that involved training and showing our dogs at local fairs. But when Dutchess (a mutt) beat her purebred Doberman at the county fair *and* won grand champion, our friendship faltered, and she took Marnie with her. They started a campaign to nickname me Penny Poodle, and I started seeing "Penny + Spot (K9)" written on desks and lockers all around school.

Phys ed class was especially difficult because I was the only girl who hadn't "become a woman" by starting menstruating. The teasing was relentless. You might wonder how they knew I hadn't started getting visits from Aunt Flo. It was obvious if you were on the rag (another lovely moniker): instead of a shower in front of all the other girls, you got to take a sponge bath. This was essentially using a damp cloth to wipe yourself down in the privacy of a bathroom stall after gym. I never had to do that.

Maybe it was the fallout from my earlier life of crime that dissuaded me from being able to just lie and take the sponge bath once a month, which was what my mom told me to do. Mom didn't really have much sympathy for me; she couldn't understand why I was so upset about not starting my period. "It's awful! You're lucky, and they are probably just jealous," she told me. It didn't seem like they were jealous, though.

Most of the students harassed me endlessly, except for the two overweight girls who were also targets. One day my panties were stolen out of my locker and run up the flagpole. I knew telling my teacher about it was probably a bad move, but I did it anyway—and then got to sit through her lecture to the whole class. "Penny had to return *with her mother* to get her panties back," she admonished them. I hadn't. I went back later by myself, or maybe my sister went with me—I can't even remember who accompanied me on the walk of shame. I just remember I wasn't willing to pull them down at the end of the school day while all the kids were milling around! Anyway, things did get better after that, even though I went from being Penny Poodle to being a rat for tattling.

This all may sound trivial, but as a teenager with raging hormones, I felt tortured. And in the eighth grade, I first started thinking about ending my life. I tried to tell my mom I felt like something was really wrong with me, but she was dismissive and said I was just having "growing pains." In later years, she expressed much regret over not taking my teen angst more seriously. Early counseling may have thwarted my attempts to find happiness and acceptance through other, self-destructive means. Then again, I wouldn't be who I am today without having survived the bullying.

I went off to high school, which was like starting a new life. In our small town, there were two junior highs that converged into one high school, and there, I found plenty of new people who had no knowledge of my shameful past. So I wasn't popular—the measure by which all teenage girls determine their self-esteem—but I had friends, and it was fun for the most part. Oh, and my period finally started, so, yay?

At the beginning of junior year, I not only had great friends but also a major crush on a drummer in the school band, who I thought might like me back. Things were looking good. But then my dad retired, and we packed up and moved to Bend, Oregon.

Living in Oregon was a shit show in many ways. We lived far out in the country, which was a huge change from being able to just walk out our door and down the street to get a burger at Kow Korner in Oak Harbor. The culture was very different from a military town, and it felt like we had just moved out to the boondocks. The house we rented was small, meaning Laura and I had to share a room, and we were now far enough into our teen years to despise each other. Along with my changing hormones, I had also begun to experience emotional problems. One night when my parents were out, I got in a screaming fight with Laura and Brad. They were ganging up on me, and the trauma from the bullying of my younger years bubbled up. I retreated to the bathroom in an effort to escape them. What happened after that was (and still is) a blur. I only know I burst out of the bathroom and ran to the kitchen, where I grabbed a butcher knife and chased my sister out into the snow, threatening to kill her.

Don't worry, I didn't. I finally calmed down, and afterward, felt so dissociated from the event that I couldn't recognize the severity of the situation. My parents did, though, and my mom threatened to send me to boarding school if I didn't shape up. I was able to tone it down for a while, but that was just the first of many times I would lose control of my emotions.

I hated Bend, my family hated Bend, and it seemed as if

Bend hated my family. One night, an evil man, who lived next door and had been causing trouble with other neighbors, stole our dog, Charlie, and dumped him somewhere far away. We got him back, but when the neighbor stole him a second time, right around Christmas, we never found him again. The guy was nuts. He even shot at us when we were out in our front yard making "too much noise." Between the dognapping and the constant threat of violence, my mom plunged into a deep depression and would lie on the couch all day. Desperate to bring normalcy back to our family, my dad made the decision for us to return to Oak Harbor.

Life improved immensely after our return to Washington. Mom's depression cleared up almost immediately, and I went back to my beloved high school. I became a choir geek and thrived socially, if not academically. At first, I hung out with my same old friends, but eventually I joined the self-titled "other" group, named such because we felt we were misfits who didn't fit into the two major categories of cliques. There were the "jocks," the popular kids (whether or not they excelled in sports), and the "hoods," the bad kids who hung out in the smoking area, smoked pot, and drank alcohol on the weekend.

The worst thing our group ever engaged in was cutting class, me more often than the rest of them. Partying was something none of us "others" were really interested in doing. Well, except for when my friends Tori and Betsy and I mixed a variety of alcohol from Tori's parents' liquor cabinet and went to the last dance of the year completely plastered. I passed out under a table and suffered a very regrettable three-day hangover. Other than that, my senior year was blessedly uneventful. Although, I almost didn't complete school due to my propensity for skipping class. But in 1980, at seventeen years of age, I graduated high school.

CHAPTER 3

GOING HOME

When you're a young adult in a town that only has one the-ater and a roller rink for entertainment, you want to get the fuck out of there as fast as you can. Though I was interested in dating, there weren't really many prospects except for dumb high school boys, yucky older boys who hadn't left for college, and sailors, whom we had been sternly warned about—even though most of the girls I knew had one for a father, myself included. It was no secret that most high school dropouts were girls who'd become pregnant as the result of a tryst with some squid, which is how we referred to the sailors. Besides, my dream was to be a rock singer, and even though I hadn't quite figured out how I would make that happen, I knew it wasn't going to happen in Oak "Joke" Harbor.

The opportunity for me to leave came almost immediately after high school ended; Tori needed a sidekick for her trip to Florida. Her parents were moving there in just a few months, when her dad would be retiring from the military, and they thought it was a good idea to send Tori ahead to live with her aunt and uncle. Once her parents arrived, the plan was for us to move in with them. A month after we graduated, my dad taught us how to change a flat tire on her little lime-green VW Rabbit, and we were on our way. The trip was a blast—well, except for my first speeding ticket, which I got in Kansas. A state, by the way, that's so flat you can practically see from one end to the other. The drive is so mundane that speeding is almost unavoidable. After a week of driving, with some stops along the way to sightsee, we arrived in Indiantown, Florida, thirty miles west of Palm Beach.

Living in Florida was not as ideal as I had anticipated; it was actually miserable. I liked Tori's aunt and her cousins just fine, but for some reason, her uncle didn't care for me. He constantly got on my case for stupid stuff, like whenever I hummed a tune. The dude seemed to hate me, and the feeling was mutual. Along with that, this town was so small it made Oak Harbor look like a metropolis. The only work I could find was a waitressing job at a tiny little café. Before I even started my first shift, I called my mom and begged for help to get me back home. She was only willing to spring for a Greyhound bus ticket, but I had no other choice. I took her up on the offer. Although I initially dreaded being surrounded by strangers on a smelly old bus, I met a number of interesting people on that five-day journey, and I didn't hate the experience. I felt like I was on my own and independent for the first time. Back at home, it wasn't long before I was itching to leave once more. I just couldn't buy into Dorothy's "there's no place like home" theory. I was always searching for happiness somewhere else.

***

Years later, my patient Don did not feel the same; he desperately wanted to go home. A forty-seven-year-old former UPS driver and single father to a ten-year-old son, Don was diagnosed with a cancer that had metastasized to his brain, and he was in the last days to weeks of his life.

It was June and the weather was crappy, as had been the case for the whole month so far. Gray skies and pouring-down rain. Not a good day for driving and definitely not a good day to be traveling across the country in a rented motor home with a dying man in the back. Still, Don's sister, Danny, was intent on taking him back to her home in Ohio, despite his declining condition. I had only cared for Don for three days, and it was my responsibility on this Sunday to see him off. When I first heard of this madness, I was incredulous beyond belief. "They're taking him *where*? In *what*?!" It was a request I had not ever heard in my more-than-five years working in hospice. I was doubtful we could make this happen, and even if we could, I was fearful of what could lie ahead for this family. It seemed like the kind of wish that could only be granted by a magical heel click, and I didn't see that happening anytime soon.

Don was unable to stand or walk. The caved-in right side of his head was testimony to the brain surgery that left him with no use of the left side of his body and little use of the right. His main complaint was pain, and he had lots of it. Methadone around the clock helped to ease his suffering. But the development of a blood clot in his right leg escalated his agony on the morning of his departure and demanded multiple doses of morphine to control the searing pain.

Don was obviously a popular guy with his former UPS coworkers and friends. There were constant visitors bringing goodies, massages, and kindness. The atmosphere in his room was often party-like, with beer free-flowing for all. Even though it was a healthcare facility, we did make exceptions for patients and visitors to toss a few back as long as they didn't cause trouble. I knew all too well the fine line between having a good time partying and getting into trouble. At times I was forced to put aside my personal judgments and watch as Don downed his methadone with a glass of German beer. *After all,* I thought, *what's the worst that could happen? He might die? He's already dying.*

My nonchalance would change in the next couple of days as Don's confusion increased and I worried about an acceleration of symptoms that could complicate the already risky journey. It's doubtful the narcotic-alcohol combo is what led to his confusion. After all, he did have brain cancer. Nevertheless, on the morning of his departure, I suggested that perhaps water or juice would be a better choice of beverage during the voyage. Just in case.

I sat down with Danny and her husband and began my final instructions with them. It was my desire to impart them with every possible bit of information they might need to deal with any situation that could arise when transporting a dying patient in a motor home for three days. Before I began my prepared speech, I recalled a scene I had witnessed the day before.

Danny was on her cell phone, discussing the details of the motor home rental with her husband. She cupped her hand lightly over the phone. "They got the biggest one. It's brand new. It still has a new smell to it," she said to Don, smiling. Don reached his hand out to Danny—high five! It was a moment that touched my heart beyond belief. I saw my own brother in that instant, and I knew if it were him in that bed, I would also do whatever it took to carry out his last desire. His dying wish.

"First of all, I want you to know how much I can appreciate your decision to do this, and I support you one hundred percent," I began. "I don't want to scare you, but as a nurse, I would be remiss if I didn't prepare you for some very real possibilities that could occur during your trip." They listened intently as I began to discuss the end-of-life symptoms and how they could be managed in an emergency. Finally, I said out loud to them what I knew we were all thinking, "It's a very real possibility that Don could die while you are traveling."

The determined look on Danny's face juxtaposed with tears that rolled down her cheeks revealed both her resolve and her trepidation. As we hugged before leaving the little meeting room, she clung to me tightly. I wanted to tell her what I really thought: *Wait, don't go today . . . Just give it another day and see what happens.* I knew what her response to that suggestion would be, so I didn't bother making it. The motor home was rented, the moving crew was assembled, Don was ready. There would be no delays.

I medicated Don heavily with morphine and lorazepam before we began the transfer. I had already scoped out the motor home and plotted our path. The door was narrow, the hall only slightly wider. It would be tricky and even possibly dangerous. I asked everyone to leave Don's room; I had no desire to turn the event into a circus. There would be enough pandemonium once we reached the parking lot and proceeded with the most difficult part of the transfer.

Before we started, I leaned over Don and stroked his forehead as I softly spoke into his ear. "I'm so sorry, Don, but I'm going to be honest. This will hurt, and there's not much we can do to make it any less painful. But we will get it over with as quickly as we can." With the aid of a mechanical lift, two nursing assistants, and another nurse, we were able to place Don in a reclining wheelchair. The transfer was arduous, and he suffered much pain. He yelled repeatedly as we carefully rolled him back and forth, getting the lift sling into position. Once Don was seated in the sling, we hoisted him into the air and gently placed him in the wheelchair. With phase one completed, we were ready for the most daunting task.

I wheeled Don out to the parking lot, where the motor home and half a dozen strapping, off-duty UPS drivers awaited. With all that brute strength available, I would be free to direct the transfer. We formed an assembly line. Three men passed Don through the narrow opening of the motor home, to the receiving crew, who gingerly placed him on a single bed in the main living area. From there, the two strongest of the bunch carried Don down the narrow hallway and into the master bed in the back. I was able to maintain my calm during the process, but inside, I was petrified. The transfer was hard on Don, but he didn't complain. Once we settled him into the bed, I instructed Danny which medications to give him so he could rest in comfort. Hugs and expressions of gratitude were shared by all of us. It was an amazing process, and I felt fortunate to have been part of that special team.

Several days later, we received a call from a hospice in Ohio. It seemed that Danny had called ahead after encountering some problems during the trip. They were expecting Don's arrival for admission. We heard nothing else until a few weeks later when Danny called to let us know Don was still alive and doing fine. He was spending his last days in the company of his sister's family and his ten-year-old son. He had made it home.

***

Once I got back home from my brief and disappointing visit to Florida, I found employment as an egg picker at a poultry farm. You heard that right, I picked eggs for a living. It was the first real job I'd had since my brief employment as a daffodil picker during the summer break before senior year. That job had an untimely ending when I was fired for my stems being too short. You heard that right too. *Insert eye roll here.*

Oak Harbor was still a boring tiny town, but I soon befriended another alumna, Danielle, and we found fun cruising the streets night after night, fraternizing with some men who had graduated a few years before us. I had blossomed from an acne-faced, ugly adolescent into a bombshell young woman and was now more interesting to and interested in finding men. Although neither Danielle nor I felt like the civilian boys were good prospects, we continued to hang out with them. They were able to get us booze, and with my first, puke-filled outcome from drinking alcohol over a year behind me, I soon found I enjoyed inebriation very much. And then we discovered two things that would elevate our party game. One, that sailors weren't as bad as we had been led to believe, and two, that there was a nightclub for those enlisted in the navy and their guests, where we could party into the wee hours of the night.

We went to the club as often as I could talk Danielle into it. She was much more of a homebody than I was, but I could get her to go along most of the time. There we would dance all night and drink rum-and-Cokes concealed from the security guards in chimney glasses. Our beverages were purchased for us by whichever sailor was trying to get into our pants, but plying us with alcohol never worked. At nineteen years old, Danielle and I prided ourselves on still having our virginity. The best part of those nights was being able to sing a song with whatever band was playing. I did, after all, still want to become a rock star.

Even with all the attention I was getting at the club, my contentment after returning home from Florida was waning and my wanderlust was growing. This time, my searching would take me to bustling Jewett City, Connecticut, where, my friend Sherry assured me, I would be able to find fame.

Sherry and I worked together at the poultry farm. She was twenty-four and had just moved out to Washington with her thirteen-month-old boy, Teddy, whom I adored. Even though Sherry was five years older than I was, we became fast friends.

Sherry had come out to the West Coast on the advice of her sister. They didn't seem to get along very well, so I'm not sure why she thought it was a good move. Now a year later, she apparently felt differently than I about where her happiness was and decided she wanted to go back home to Connecticut. We had become great friends, or so I thought. As I later found out, she really just needed a ride, and I was foolish enough to buy into her grandiose proclamation that if I wanted to make it as a singer, Jewett City was the place to be.

We packed up my Subaru BRAT and away we went. The trip wasn't unlike the one I had made to Florida, except for the toddler in between us and that we were poor and slept in the car instead of stopping at motels. We made it to our final destination in about five or six days, if I remember correctly. Truthfully, I try to forget that trip—both the move and the horrible person Sherry turned out to be.

Almost immediately after we arrived, the whole situation became a nightmare. We stayed with relatives of Sherry's for a few weeks until we both secured jobs working in a factory. Then we moved into a shitty apartment in the slums. Sherry went out drinking every night, leaving me to babysit Teddy. That was fine by me, because when she was around, she was mean to us both. Before too long, I found an ad for someone looking for a roommate on the break room bulletin board. Donna had a big house and two little boys and needed someone to help her with the rent. As much as I hated leaving Teddy alone, I couldn't tolerate Sherry's bullshit anymore and moved in with Donna right away. Well, out of the frying pan and into the fire . . .

It's hard to say who was really the worst of those two. Donna was fine at first, but her parenting skills were lacking as much as Sherry's. At the time, I thought her three-year-old, Joey, was just a willful brat. Every morning, I would get up before Donna and find the kitchen a disaster. Joey would have dumped several two-liter bottles of soda on the floor, cereal would be spilled everywhere. One time he tried to cook a package of spaghetti—plastic bag and all. I discovered it just as the plastic was starting to melt and catch on fire. Looking back on this years later, I realized the poor kid was just hungry.

Donna stole from me: clothes, makeup, jewelry, and my checkbook, which she used to bounce checks all over town. I didn't want to be held responsible for all the bad checks, so I reported her to the police. That enraged and incited her to make my already miserable life even more hellish. She was connected to local law enforcement through her brother-in-law and used them to carry out her vendetta against me. They couldn't get me for the bad checks, since I had already proved the signatures weren't mine. So instead, they came after me for failure to change the tabs on my license plates from Washington to Connecticut. There wasn't much they could do but issue warnings due to a grace period I hadn't yet exceeded. Still, being pulled over constantly was intimidating and stressful.

I realized I had to get out of there fast, and not just out of Donna's house—out of Connecticut. I had certainly not found happiness or fame there, and I was ready to go home. I was able to leave Donna's house and moved in with a boy I had met at the factory who was head over heels in love with me. The feelings weren't mutual, and I didn't intend to stay with him long. I was up-front about that with him, though; I didn't want to feel like I was using him, even though I kind of was. After getting my final paycheck from the factory, my plan was to buy some NoDoz (over-the-counter anti-sleeping pills), jump in my BRAT, and drive until I got back home.

The day I was planning to leave, I woke up to find a busted-out windshield on my car. Somehow, even though I had recently moved where supposedly no one knew where I was, Donna or one of her cronies found me and had hurled a massive rock through my windshield. Feeling defeated and now without a solid plan, I called my mom. Again.

Despite all the drama, I had not talked to my parents at all. I didn't want to worry them, but that appeared to have backfired. My lack of communication had caused them so much concern that my mom was about to notify the authorities.

"Oh my God, I've been so worried about you!" Mom said, her voice breaking. She told me she needed to think about what to do and would call me back. An hour later, she called and told me to go to the Western Union in Jewett City, pick up the hundred dollars she had wired, and take the car across the street to an auto shop. They would be expecting me, and she'd already paid them to repair my window. "Once the window is fixed," she said, "drive out of town as far as you can safely go before you get too tired, stop at a motel, and then call home." She didn't need to tell me twice.

Staring at the road through my brand-new windshield with a gaze as fixed as that of a dying person, I headed out of that fucking town as fast as I could. Actually, I was driving under the speed limit and looking in my rearview mirror constantly, because after having been pulled over so often, I felt like a fugitive. Once I stopped for the night, I called home as I had been instructed. My sister answered, saying, "Mom is on her way to the airport." The next morning, I met my mom at the airport in Scranton, Pennsylvania, and in January, during the quiet dead of winter, we made the long journey back to Oak Harbor together.

I've moved many more times since then, mostly due to my affiliation with the military through past husbands. Moving so often didn't really offer the opportunity to be satisfied where I was. But at some point in my life, I finally realized that happiness can't be found just by changing your location, and home is a pretty great place to be.

Okay, Dorothy, you win.

CHAPTER 4

THE IMPACT OF DRUGS AND ALCOHOL ON LIFE

My drinking had continued in Connecticut, but due to the ongoing crisis I was enduring, it wasn't as prevalent as it had been before my move. That changed almost immediately once I returned to my stomping grounds. I resumed my friendship with Danielle, who forgave me for leaving her behind and helped me get a job at the Navy Exchange. We also resumed partying, and little by little I started emulating the classic alcoholic, creating wreckage in my life.

The first time I went to jail was for the dumbest thing; not that the other times were the result of brilliance. Danielle and I were drinking beer at a state park with some sailors, and a park ranger busted us. The sailors got tickets for buying us the booze, and Danielle and I were ticketed for illegal consumption of alcohol by a minor. She was smart and paid for her ticket right away. I, however, had not yet learned the valuable lesson of consequences and decided not to pay it. A year later Danielle and I were hanging out at the beach again with different sailors, and a couple of cops decided to see what we were up to. They ran our licenses and lo and behold, there was a bench warrant for my arrest. Off to jail I went until the next morning, when Danielle bailed me out.

I would like to say I was more careful after that, but really, it was more like dumb luck. I continued to drink frequently and heavily but didn't find myself in any more legal trouble—for a while anyway. It wasn't just alcohol I used to alter my mind either. I pretty much did whatever drug was put in front of me. I dabbled in a plethora of mind-altering substances, from LSD to magic mushrooms, hash, and pot. I think meth was around in those days, but thankfully, I was never presented with the opportunity to try it, because I'm sure that would not have ended well. I had my druggie friends, who were civilians, and my alcohol buddies, who were sailors, and between those two groups, I never wanted for a good time.

I went back to the Navy club, back to belting out Pat Benatar songs with the bands, back to dancing all night, and was again very popular with the men. I ate up the attention, but underneath my exuberant personality was a growing darkness. The first time it overwhelmed me to the point of self-harm, I had been drinking heavily. I intentionally drove my dad's truck into a tree. I was not hurt, probably because I was so wasted, but my dad's truck needed repair. Lucky for me, one of my party buddies managed an auto parts store and helped me out. I told my parents I had swerved to avoid hitting a deer and was praised for "doing the right thing," as hitting a deer could have been much worse. Did I feel guilty about that? Not really. I was far from being able to experience any kind of humility during that time of my life.

It was an eye-opener, though; I could have killed myself for real. Once that darkness had peaked, the light returned, and I continued to drink, and drug, and drink, and drug. Oh, and have sex. I had lost my virginity in Connecticut to the guy who had let me stay with him. I didn't love him, but I felt obligated, since he had been so helpful and kind to me when I needed to get the hell out of there.

So now, without the pride of chastity, I became more

willing to put out, earning me more attention from men. Though, I actually only slept with a couple of men before I hooked up with Bruce, the first love of my life. Bruce was a sailor, of course. We had met at the club one night. He was a good dancer, a guitar player with aspirations of being a professional musician, very good-looking, and very, *very* good in bed. He was also an arrogant jerk who liked to make me pay my own way whenever we went out.

The first time it happened, we were out with Danielle and her new boyfriend at a cafeteria. Bruce was in line in front of me and paid for his food but not mine. I was mortified. I had no money. I turned to Danielle, and she poked her boyfriend, who jumped in front of me and paid for the meals for all three of us. You would think that would have been the end of me and Bruce, but for some reason, I continued to be with him. Positive attention from men and the knowledge that I had bloomed since high school notwithstanding, I carried the burden of low self-esteem. And there's nothing like low self-esteem to keep you in a relationship with an asshole. We started talking about getting married and moving to California. But that was going to have to wait because he was about to be deployed on a nine-month cruise.

I played the loyal girlfriend for a few months after he left. I sent him letters and care packages. Danielle's boyfriend was on the same cruise, and she and I even participated in events with the wives of the other sailors on the ship. I was in love, and I thought the feelings were mutual until the tone of Bruce's letters started to change.

"Maybe we should just live together first," he wrote. Then a few letters later, "I should probably go to California first." I did not like the proverbial handwriting I was seeing on the wall. I became sure that Bruce was going to dump me.

Danielle was much better than I was at coping with her boyfriend's absence. She was still a homebody and didn't have any issue with staying in every night. But I couldn't stay at home; the party persona I had grown into wouldn't allow it. Without my drinking buddy, I found a new group of men to hang out with, and one of them was Lenny, a sailor, of course. After yet another night of drinking way too much and feeling dejected by yet another Dear Jane letter, I let things go a little too far with Lenny. He was wasted, as was I, and he kept telling me he wanted to get me pregnant so I would have to marry him. This flattered my waning ego, and suffice to say, mission accomplished.

When I realized I was pregnant, I was filled with regret. I was in no way prepared to give up my lifestyle of partying, and I especially didn't want to marry someone I barely knew. One day I told him I was thinking I should get an abortion.

"If you don't want my child," he told me angrily, "you don't want me." The truth was that I didn't want him, but shame kept me from admitting that, so I made plans for our wedding. My mom had made it clear that if I was to have a baby, I was to get married.

With our baby on the way, Lenny made the good decision to reenlist, which came with a move to a new station. Being a military family stacked the odds more in our favor for adulting. There was a consistent paycheck, medical care, dental care, and access to the Navy Exchange and commissary where we could buy food and clothes at a fraction of the cost in civilian stores. Soon the wedding was over, and we were on our way to California. We hadn't even made it to our new home before I realized what a mistake it had been to marry him.

We were driving separate vehicles, me in the new used vehicle we had acquired, a red Mercury Bobcat station wagon with wood-paneled sides, and him in my trusty Subaru BRAT. Our new puppy, J. D., and my cats, Kyra and Pookie, rode with me. We stopped at a rest area and got in a screaming fight over something I can't for the life of me remember. But I'm sure it was stupid, because all our fights were. Finally, he jumped into the BRAT and left. He just drove away! There I was with our animals and my big, six-month baby bump alone somewhere in the mountains in Oregon. I was terrified. We didn't have cell phones or GPS back then. I had no idea where I was. After about half an hour, he returned, hugged me, and apologized. I was still pissed and didn't want to forgive him, but I was also relieved to not be alone, so I gave him a quick hug back and we headed south again.

We found a little house to rent in Escondido, and I began to do that thing all pregnant women supposedly do—nest. I spent my time doing retail therapy with the hefty bonus he received for his reenlistment, and for a while that placated the sadness I had over leaving my social life behind. On September 26, 1983, we welcomed Keith Joseph after a grueling thirty-eight-hour labor ending in a C-section. Back then, ultrasounds did not produce the high-quality images they do these days, where the detail is so granular you can agree which parent the baby resembles more before they are even born. We didn't do gender-reveal parties; the sex was revealed when the baby was. I spent my pregnancy wishing for a girl. So much so that when one of the labor and delivery nurses told me the heart rate was fast, which meant I was probably carrying a boy, I was truly bummed. But the moment the doctor announced, "It's a boy," as he placed the baby next to my head, I felt immediate relief.

"I'm so happy he's a boy," I sobbed to Lenny, "because if he wasn't a boy, he wouldn't be Keith." In my mind, this little human already had a personality. I snuggled my face to his. I instantly loved him. I wanted to stay close to him like that forever. And then I felt a warm sensation shoot through the needle in my wrist into my vein, and I was out cold.

My body has never been amenable to birthing babies. I've had issues with every child. When Keith was born, the epidural required for the surgery caused a condition called a spinal headache, which had to be treated with a blood patch, an injection of my own blood into my spine, and twenty-four hours flat on my back. This was a critical time just after birth when I should have been able to bond with my baby, but I was denied that opportunity. Prior to his birth, I hadn't taken any Lamaze or other birthing classes, so I was completely unprepared for the birth experience and didn't know how to breastfeed. Once I was able to sit up again and hold Keith, I tried nursing him. He immediately chomped down on my nipple, causing searing pain. Having never been educated to expect this (lactation consultants weren't even a thing back then), I didn't understand that this was him latching on to me, not him biting me. I couldn't tolerate the pain and decided the bottle would be a better way to go.

Despite the issues and constant tiredness that plague all new parents, I loved Keith so much. He was so beautiful—he actually looked like a clone of my own baby pictures. He had just the right amount of dark hair, and dark-brown eyes. And he was an easy baby, not at all colicky, as one of his future sisters would be. But something else was happening to me at that time.

I had not yet been diagnosed with obsessive-compulsive disorder (OCD) and wouldn't be for years. But I had experienced one of its symptoms, intrusive bad thoughts, for as long as I could remember. The types of thoughts I had were things like talking to someone with a cup of coffee in my hand and having the urge to fling it in their face, holding a kitten and thinking about squeezing the life out of it, or driving over a bridge and getting a feeling like I wanted to steer my car off of it. Of course, these were thoughts I would *never* act on, and intrusive thoughts aren't really something you consciously think of anyway. I used to have a hard time explaining exactly what they were, so I didn't ever talk about it to people. I was sure they would give me the side-eye and say, "You want to do what now?"

It wasn't until years after Keith was born that I was watching some show that featured a woman describing her OCD symptoms. She said she was sitting next to the fireplace one night, holding her newborn, and she could envision herself throwing her baby into the fire. That brought me some relief—I knew I wasn't alone with this experience, and I felt I could tell someone now. That someone was my mom. She told me about her own intrusive thoughts, like one that would occur when she was cutting babies' fingernails and cause her to envision herself snipping their fingertips off. *Note to self: remember to tell Mom to put the nail clippers down and step away from my baby!* I didn't worry, though, because I understood her and that those thoughts were as troubling to her as mine were to me. And she, just like me, never would have acted on them. After I confided in Mom about this dreadful affliction, learning we weren't alone was liberating for both of us. We quickly asked my sister if she had the same kind of thoughts. She stared at us blankly. I guess not.

But learning that OCD didn't make me a potential cat murderer or terrible driver didn't come about until years after Keith was born. Back then, I had a vulnerable little person in my care, and my intrusive thoughts were so much worse, so much more disturbing. I would be holding Keith in the middle of the night, and as I stood up to place him back in his cradle, I would envision myself dropping my arms and letting him fall onto the hard floor. It horrified me and added to my increasing insecurities and self-doubt about my ability to be a parent.

In addition, as I pretty much had expected it would be, my marriage to Lenny was a disaster. I didn't love him, I didn't respect him, and I didn't want to have sex with him, which was a major source of argument. In his frustration, he began to drink heavily, and when he did, he was an abusive asshole. Once the abuse started, I realized this could be my ticket out of the marriage. I waited until he had been drinking, started an argument, and once he was riled up enough and drunk enough, I goaded him into hitting me.

"Hit me, then," I would scream at him when he was worked up, and he would. On one occasion, the cops even showed up at our house after the neighbors reported my screaming and his yelling. After about two years of this madness, I finally called my mom and begged her to come and get me. A few weeks later, she and I packed up as many of my worldly belongings as we could fit in my station wagon, and, of course, Keith. We headed back to Washington, leaving behind Lenny and our pets (now two cats and two dogs). I never regretted leaving Lenny, but I felt guilt and regret over abandoning my pets, all of whom ended up in the animal shelter, most likely euthanized. I am now embarrassed to say I did not feel the same remorse later when I abandoned my son.

CHAPTER 5

THE IMPACT OF DRUGS AND ALCOHOL ON DEATH

Many people, patients, families, and even some medical professionals express fear around the use of morphine at the end of a person's life. They truly believe it is what will ultimately take a dying person out. I can't tell you how many times internet trolls have left nasty comments on my videos accusing hospice nurses of murdering our patients by giving them morphine. There is also worry from families about addiction.

Both concerns are unfounded. We start morphine (or any opioids, for that matter) at small, safe doses and increase them incrementally as needed. Incidentally, all opioids have the potential ability to cause death or addiction, but for some reason, it's morphine that has a bad reputation. These drugs are given for a specific reason, the reason they were developed for: symptom management. I always tell people who are concerned about addiction that we are using the meds for their intended purpose, not recreationally for party time. While keeping people comfortable at the end of life often means needing to increase the pain medication as they adjust to the dose, that isn't addiction. Although we do use other opioids besides morphine, it's still the primary drug used for symptom management. It's inexpensive and the gold standard for effective management of pain and shortness of breath.

Interestingly, though people are afraid of the use of a doctor-prescribed medication at the end of life, they are fascinated to learn about the ability to drink alcohol or smoke cigarettes or weed while on hospice. Anytime I post a video on social media explaining or even alluding to hospice patients being allowed to have a cocktail, it goes viral. In "normal" healthcare settings, alcohol is frowned upon or even prohibited, but in end-of-life care, we take a different stance. If someone wants to enjoy their favorite alcoholic beverage, that's fine with us. After all, for many people, happy hour plays an important role in quality of life. This is evidenced by the popularity of the videos where I say go ahead! Of course, the caveat is that we want patients to imbibe safely, so we will have a conversation about the potential dangers of mixing alcohol with benzodiazepines or narcotic medications.

As far as other mind-altering recreational substances go, marijuana typically isn't a problem, but we still want disclosure about it just in case there are any concerns about its use with prescribed meds (there usually aren't). We do have to draw a line if we learn other, harder drugs, such as meth, heroin, and so on, are being used. These illegal drugs not only come with a risk to the person using, but also to our clinicians going into that type of environment. Learning someone is participating in the use of those risky drugs could potentially cause them to be discharged from hospice.

Many families seem to be most concerned about their person smoking cigarettes, especially in cases where their disease was caused by cigarettes in the first place. My opinion? That ship has more than sailed—it's been sunk. The only result you'll see from forcing a dying smoker not to smoke is to make them and everyone around them miserable. Our main concern if someone wants to smoke is if oxygen is in use. This could, and has on many occasions, caused fires or even explosions. Otherwise, smoke 'em if you got 'em! Regulating the use of tobacco, drugs, and alcohol is not as relevant at the end of life. It's during the rest of your life that overindulgence can come with some significant consequences.

One morning, just after I arrived at the nurses' station of the hospice care center, I heard screams coming from the room next door. I went in to find Shannon, my RN partner, and a woman in a hospital gown in a standoff. They were on opposite sides of the hospital bed. Shannon was nearest to the door, standing in an almost relaxed posture, leaning back slightly with hands crossed below her waist, head tilted to the side.

"I know what you're trying to do, and you won't get away with it!" Margaret, the patient, said menacingly. She held a coffee cup in her hand, but not for long because without warning, she flung it toward her nurse. Shannon ducked as it flew past her.

"Oops, missed!" she said casually. I almost thought she seemed a little amused, which didn't strike me as unusual, since Shannon had a way of taking a lighthearted approach in every interaction with her patients, good or bad. I was more surprised Margaret was being so aggressive with Shannon, who, at six feet tall, had a calm but commanding demeanor most people found intimidating. Most people in their right mind, that is, but unfortunately, many disease processes cause people to become, shall we say, unhinged.

Margaret suffered from end-stage cirrhosis of the liver caused by her overindulgence in alcoholic beverages. She had only arrived at the care center a few days earlier, for symptom management but also due to her overall growing needs as the progression of her disease exceeded her ability to live alone. Aside from alcoholism being the cause of her terminal condition, it was also the cause of a fractured relationship with her family, leaving her with no caregivers.

A serious problem with any liver disease is that it can increase ammonia levels in the brain, which leads to confusion or even severe psychosis. There is a treatment for this very troubling symptom, a disgustingly sweet, syrupy medication called Lactulose. Not only does it taste bad, it works by causing the person to shit out the toxins. And when I say "shit," I mean as in shit their brains out. This is a side effect most patients cannot tolerate, and, understandably, they usually choose to stop the treatment. Anyway, Margaret was beyond Lactulose at this point, even if she would willingly drink it. Her psychosis was in full swing.

Some may be surprised by this, but working in hospice, and healthcare in general, is not without risk of violence from patients. A hospice nurse must learn to manage an out-of-control patient and stay safe while maintaining some level of compassion. We have to keep in mind that our patients may have no control over their actions. I once saw Shannon sit quietly next to an angry man with an altered mental status who was holding on to her wrist tightly while he yelled at her to let him go. "You're holding *my* hand," she calmly said to him, not even trying to wriggle away.

Later, I began to put into practice what I had learned from Shannon, when an angry dementia patient grabbed me by the lapels of my scrubs and began to shake me violently. I held his hands firmly and calmly told him, through gritted teeth, that he needed to "let *go* of my new jacket!" I had paid a pretty penny for my *Grey's Anatomy* designer lab coat, and I would be damned if it would get ripped the first day I wore it! The hospice aide at the bedside with me was incredulous at my response.

"That guy was shaking you like a rag doll, and you were more concerned about your clothes," she said, laughing. She was so impressed, and amused, by my actions that she re-counted the incident to anyone who would listen for years. The story of "Nurse Penny's precious lab coat" became almost leg-endary at the care center.

Now, once again, we were faced with a confused and agi-tated patient. Without turning away from Margaret, Shannon somehow sensed my presence behind her.

"Can you go see what we have for her?" she asked me qui-etly. At this point in my hospice career, and having worked under Shannon's tutelage for the past year, I knew what she was instructing me to do. I bounded out of the room for the nurses' station. It only took me seconds to reach the locked med room door, and after quickly punching in the key code, I swung the door open and grabbed the medication administra-tion record, or MAR, as we referred to it. I flipped through the book until I landed on the section with our patient's name on it.

"Haldol," I almost yelled out. I realized adrenaline had me amped up a little bit, and I took a breath to calm myself down.

Haloperidol, or Haldol by brand name, is an antipsy-chotic medication typically used for mental health disorders. For hospice patients, it also works very well for several com-mon symptoms, such as nausea, hallucinations, and agitation, which is what I hoped it could treat for Margaret. However, the order was for a topical gel we had to rub onto our patient's wrist, where it would absorb over time. This form worked fine for less urgent needs, such as nausea, but I knew it wouldn't be great for the level of agitation Margaret was experiencing. Still, it was all I had available at the moment, and Dr. Bower, the doc of the day, was nowhere to be found. *Hopefully this will buy us a little time,* I thought as I squirted the ordered dose into a plastic med cup.

By the time I returned, Shannon had made her way over to Margaret and was calmly holding one of her hands. "We're not trying to hurt you," she said to her in a soothing alto. Margaret squirmed feebly, trying to get free from Shannon's grip, but in her weakened state, her efforts were useless. I grabbed a pair of gloves from the holder on the wall and pulled them on as I updated Shannon.

"Sorry, the doctor wasn't anywhere near the station, and I figured this would be better than nothing," I explained. I walked over to where the women stood and positioned myself behind Shannon, where Margaret wouldn't see what was coming. I reached around and slathered the gel on her wrist, rubbing it in quickly. "Okay," I said quietly to Shannon, "I'm sure this isn't going to do much, but maybe it will help a little while I go track down Dr. Bower."

As I took my leave from the room, I thought about my own trials with alcoholism. "There but for the grace of God go I" was a saying I picked up in a treatment center or AA meeting somewhere along the way. I understood the meaning of those words, but they didn't resonate with me until I started working in hospice. Caring for patients who weren't as fortunate as I'd been in shaking loose my addictions reminded me every day of an outcome I'd narrowly escaped. I saw patients whose lives were cut short, whose ties to their families were severed, or who missed opportunities because of the disease of addiction—and later the disease *caused by* the addiction. Patients like Margaret, for whom I often found myself hopeful that she might receive a visitor. But Margaret had no family— at least no family who cared to see her.

I returned to the nurses' station and was relieved to find the doctor seated at a table, reviewing charts. "Hey, Dr. Bower," I said as I approached him. "Margaret is super agitated, and we need some medication orders for her."

Dr. Bower looked up from the open chart in front of him and stared at me blankly over the top of his glasses. "Margaret," he said slowly, obviously trying to search his memory for whom I was referring to. "*Who* is freaking out?" he asked.

"Margaret Wilson in room six," I told him, struggling to hide my impatience. *Margaret Wilson,* I thought, irritated. *The poor woman who is dying alone, estranged from her family due to the disease of alcoholism that has destroyed her life in so many ways and is now bringing it to an end. The woman whose doctor has apparently also forgotten her!*

"The lady with cirrhosis of the liver," I stated flatly. "All she has is topical Haldol, and I just gave her a dose, but I don't think it will work for her. She's really spun up," I added, trying to convey urgency.

Dr. Bower looked back down at the chart he had been reviewing, somewhat unconcerned. "Give her some more Haldol," he directed me. "Double the dose."

I started to walk back into the med room but stopped short of the door and turned back to face him. "I think you need to come see her," I said, trying to sound confident. "I don't think topical meds are going to work." He sighed and closed the plastic binder slowly, then got up from the table. I turned around and started walking briskly back to the room. Finally sensing the urgency of the situation, he quickened his pace, catching up to me, and we entered the room side by side.

Shannon had taken hold of Margaret again. This time she stood facing her, holding both her hands in hers, but Margaret broke free and started flailing her arms. Shannon stepped back to give her some room and avoid getting hit while Margaret continued to wave her arms frantically. Her hospital gown flapped loosely about her shoulders, and she began tearing at her breasts with her nails, leaving streaks of blood. She then reached down between her legs to the tube draining urine into a bag and yanked it out. Almost instantly the look on her face changed from anger to painful disbelief, and she started to cry.

"That hurt," she sobbed. "Why do you keep hurting me?"

I winced as I saw the still-inflated balloon of the catheter she was holding up in her outstretched hand and knew how much that probably did hurt.

Dr. Bower took in the scene quietly and then turned to me. "Give her a shot of lorazepam, five milligrams in the arm." Having issued the order, Dr. Bower turned to leave the room.

Shannon took a giant step toward him. "Hold it!" she said with much irritation. "I think we're going to need a little help, don't you?"

Dr. Bower turned back around, muttering, "Oh, right."

I left the room quickly, enlivened by the chance to deliver something that would adequately calm down Margaret. I drew up the lorazepam into a syringe with a big, fat needle attached to the end, which was required to push the viscous liquid deep into the muscle. If this drug didn't do the trick to get our poor lady calmed down, nothing would.

Back in the room, Shannon and Dr. Bower slowly approached the patient, then simultaneously grabbed her arms and wrestled her to the bed. Margaret's attempts to get away were no match for Shannon and Dr. Bower, who towered over her at six-foot-four. Ever the compassionate, calm presence, Shannon leaned over, stroking the now-crying woman's hair and whispering softly into her ear, "We're not going to hurt you, we just want to help." She turned to me. "It's okay, Penny. Do it now," she said quietly.

I jabbed the long needle into Margaret's upper arm and plunged the syringe, causing her to cry out like a wounded animal. "Sorry, sorry, sorry," I apologized. Shannon and the doctor continued to subdue the woman until she began to relax. When she was finally calm, they let go of her. She stayed in bed, crying softly.

Dr. Bower left the room, and Shannon got up and turned to me, shaking her head. "Man, liver disease is a bitch," she said.

Totally, I thought, all too aware that I had narrowly avoided the possibility that I might someday need to be on the receiving end of that big, fat needle, and thankful I had repaired the relationships my drinking had damaged.

We kept Margaret comfortable by heavily sedating her, and a few days later, she died. Alone.

CHAPTER 6

THE BOTTOM OF ROCK BOTTOM

Back in Washington, I felt happy and free. Except for one thing—I wasn't truly free. I was a single mom. I would love to say I tried to be a good mom, but the hard reality is I would be blowing smoke up your ass. I wanted to party.

So, when Lenny wanted to share our son by us each having him for six months at a time, I enthusiastically agreed. This arrangement would have been undoable with Lenny still living in California, but soon after our split, he was able to plead his case to the military and get stationed back in Washington. When Keith spent his time with me, it was my mom who was his primary caretaker. I had found work as a bartender, which suited my desired lifestyle well, allowing me to be able to party and find people to party with. By the time Keith was four, I legally gave Lenny full custody of him. I would not be ready to parent Keith again until he was ten years old.

Now truly free from the responsibility of being a wife and mother, I could run as wild as I wanted, and boy, did I ever want. Although I was no stranger to drugs, there were some lines I had decided not to cross. Cocaine was one of them. My cousin Colleen, who was four years my senior and a successful journeyman welder, parlayed the lucrative paychecks from her chosen career into a cocaine habit. When she was twenty-five years old, she lost everything: her house, her car, her relationship, and then her life when she jumped to her death from the Tacoma Narrows Bridge. She never reached the water. She hit the cement pylon below and was found by a couple of horrified fishermen. At the time, I was twenty years old, very pregnant, married, living in California, and unable to attend her funeral, which was a closed casket for obvious reasons. I swore I would *never* do cocaine. And then one day, I apparently forgot my self-proclaimed vow and followed that white line down a new path.

Working in the bars enabled me to find my people: other partiers like me and ultimately my cocaine-dealing roommate, Big Jim, a larger-than-life clone of the wrestler Hulk Hogan. I began a nightly routine of drinking too much alcohol and then snorting lines of coke to sober up. This put me on a constant down-and-up emotional roller coaster where I would experience the depressing effect of the alcohol followed by the mood-uplifting effect of the cocaine.

One night as I sat in the front passenger seat of my car in front of some guy's house, the alcohol-induced depressive state I was in turned to destructive rage. I had only gone on one date with this guy, but it ended in an intimacy I felt sure meant he had already fallen in love with me, and we would live happily ever after. My friend Ellen and I had been out dancing, and I'd decided we'd go see him. She drove, because although she was drunk, I was much drunker. When we got there, I realized the car in his driveway belonged to another woman and I lost my shit. The guy was definitely not worth what I did next, but to me this was just another rejection for my already tormented soul, and the pain was unbearable.

I was decked out in a miniskirt and high heels, and my anger was augmented by my very inebriated condition. I almost felt I was an outsider looking in as, from the passenger seat, I lifted my right high-heeled foot above the dash and began kicking the windshield with every ounce of strength I could summon. Kick (smash), kick (smash), kick (smash). The small squares of glass landed on the hood of the car as if we had been caught in a hailstorm.

Ellen finally grabbed my arm. "Do you realize you're destroying your own car?" she said, somewhat amused. "You should be doing this to *his* car!"

I stopped kicking and stared blankly at her for a moment. "I don't want to end up in jail for vandalism," I said as I gave my windshield one last kick. And then I cried. I cried as I assessed the smashed window of my car. I cried as I examined the torn-up leather on my bright red heels. I cried as Ellen started the car and began to drive us away from the stupid guy and his stupid house and his stupid new girlfriend.

"I know what will make you feel better," Ellen told me. "Let's go home and see Jim."

Jim, I thought. *He has the stuff to make everything all right again.* The cocaine did not make things better, but it was always the alcohol that caused the most trouble.

On another night, I was bartending, and the dimly lit tavern was much livelier than usual for a Thursday night. But that didn't keep me from pulling out all the stops to entertain the heavily buzzed patrons. I was dressed for the occasion in typical 1980s fashion: crop top, spandex pants, and a hot-pink streak in big red hair.

I had learned early in my bartending career the best way to get better tips was to make each horny man feel like he was special. I held out one of my hands to an elderly regular and smiled provocatively. "Hey, I got a new perfume. It's called Come to Me." The man leaned over with a grin and sniffed at my wrist. I pushed it up a little closer to his nose. "Does it smell like cum to you?" The man leaned back in his chair, blushing a little while the other men at the bar burst into laughter, almost in unison. I liked giving my attention to older, married men. They were better tippers, and because they had wives at home waiting for them, their bark was always worse than their bite. I knew it was safe to flirt unabashedly without one of them thinking I would be going home with him at the end of the night.

I didn't discriminate against the younger men, though; I basked in the attention they gave me. For some reason, there seemed to be a belief that if a man was successful in getting the bartender to go out with him, it elevated his status among the other barflies. That was how I ended up dating Mitch, my abusive, alcoholic, mentally unstable boyfriend. But Mitch had been ignoring me, so when Miles started hitting on me, it boosted my waning ego.

"Hey, Penny, why don't you come sit with me after your shift and I'll buy you a drink?" he teased. I had only seen him in the bar a couple of times, but he was always nice. He was with another young-looking man, and they both seemed safe. As long as I stayed in the bar, where I was surrounded by the other staff and my "bodyguard" regulars, what could go wrong?

I requested a double whiskey, neat, from the other bartender once my shift ended. She handed me the drink, and I downed it in one shot. I held the glass out to her to pour again. "You can just use the same one. The alcohol kills my germs anyway," I said with a laugh. After grabbing the newly poured whiskey, I spun around to Miles. "Okay, let's chat a bit."

The next thing I knew, I felt tapping on my shoulder, which turned into a vigorous shake. I shrugged my arm away and groaned, feeling very annoyed. "Hey, wake up, sleepyhead. The party's not over yet," I heard a male voice say. I opened my eyes and found myself sitting in the front seat of a car between two men. Miles was in the passenger seat and his companion from the bar was driving. I blinked to clear the blurriness out of my inebriated eyes and strained to see where we were.

"Where are we going?" I asked, but as my eyes adjusted to the dark night, I recognized the trestle on the highway. "Why are we heading out of town?" I said anxiously.

The driver calmly answered, without looking away from the road. "It's cool, we're just going to Miles's house."

I was drunk, but sober enough to know this wasn't a good situation. "You need to take me back to my car *now*!" I demanded. Still not taking his eyes off the road, the driver told me to calm down, stating again that everything was cool. By this time, I was starting to get a little hysterical. "You need to pull the car over *right now*!" I reached over and pulled on the steering wheel, aiming the car toward the guardrail, where it came to a sudden crashing halt. Almost immediately, flashing blue and red lights seemed to come out of nowhere, and I felt more sober than I had at any time in my life.

Although the car had abruptly slammed into the guardrail, the two men and I seemed to be uninjured, likely because the alcohol in our systems provided a protective factor. The police car had arrived so quickly, it was almost as if they had already been tailing us. Drunk as we were, I don't think any of us immediately understood the gravity of the situation—at least I didn't. Both of the men hopped out of the car with their hands up, but I was feeling very woozy. I moved slowly as I climbed out of the car, joining the drunk men and two police officers. I could hear the driver talking to the cop, and at first I couldn't make out what he was saying. It soon became apparent he was telling the officer that I had been driving the vehicle. This infuriated me. How dare he blame me! I was a victim! As far as I was concerned, they had been in the act of kidnapping me, and I had thwarted their efforts.

I rushed up to the driver and slapped him across the face. "Stop lying!"

Miles approached me, holding his hands out defensively. "Penny, calm down."

I spun around. *"You calm down!"* I screamed.

The driver, still trying to convince the cop he was just an innocent party to the crazy woman's insanity, pointed to me. "Look, she has car keys in her hand." I looked at my clenched fist, he wasn't wrong; I was holding car keys. This confused me, but only for a moment, until I remembered where they came from.

"These are *my* keys to *my* car," I yelled. That didn't seem to matter much to the cops, and I was placed under arrest.

To this day I don't know what they charged me with. I know it wasn't assault; that came later with a domestic violence altercation. It wasn't driving under the influence. Miraculously, despite driving drunk many times, I never did get into an accident or get into any trouble for it. Maybe it was drunk and disorderly. I can't remember, or possibly subconsciously, I choose not to. Whatever it was for, they arrested me and hauled me off to jail.

The main women's jail was overloaded, so I was sat down at a desk at the police station with a bald man, who I later learned was the night-shift supervisor. The station was brightly lit, which, in my hazy mind, gave it a surreal ambiance, since it was the middle of the night. This was long before smoking indoors had become illegal, and the cop offered me a cigarette. *Marlboro Lights, my brand,* I thought approvingly. I took the cigarette and stuck it between my lips, leaning toward the flame of the lighter in the outstretched hand of my captor.

"What's your name?" I asked.

"I'm Sergeant Wilkins. You can call me Sarge. Cliché, I know, but that's what they call me around here," he told me. "But, enough about me, let's talk about what happened tonight, out there."

I explained what I could remember about the evening, which wasn't much. I paused for drags on my cigarette as I tried to gather my thoughts and, truthfully, as a bit of a delay tactic. As drunk as I was, I understood I could be put in a cell at any time, and I did my best to keep Sarge interested enough to avoid that. Although I was able to present a calm demeanor, I was feeling highly anxious inside. Even though I was in what many would consider a dire situation, my priorities, as usual, were screwed up, and my brain began to wander.

As I said, my boyfriend, Mitch, had been acting strange lately, and I felt certain he was cheating on me. I had gone out with those guys after work because his cousin Deana was having a party. I didn't get along very well with her, so I hadn't been invited—or at least that's what Mitch had told me. I didn't really like Deana either. Her best friend, Melanie, had a thing for Mitch, and Deana had been telling him he should ditch me for her. Suddenly I became suspicious the party was actually Deana's way of setting them up. My anxiety reached a tipping point.

"I get to make a phone call, right?" I burst out. "I really need to call someone now." The sergeant pushed the black push-button phone across the desk to me and informed me I could make *one* phone call.

I dialed Mitch's number and waited for it to ring. It wasn't a stretch to think Mitch was cheating on me—he had already done it within a month of us getting together. After convincing me to live with him, he cheated on me the first night we moved into our apartment. And even though he had moved out shortly afterward, I was still trying to make this highly dysfunctional and highly abusive relationship work.

The phone rang and rang. No answer. That did not bode well for my angst. I lied and told the sergeant I had got the number wrong and needed to try once more. He either fell for it or felt sorry for me, and I began dialing again. No answer. Just then, another cop entered the station and summoned the sergeant away from the desk. This gave me more opportunity to continue to dial the number. I lost track of how many times I called, but finally, I heard the click of a receiver on the other end.

"Hello?" It wasn't Mitch or Deana who answered but that trampy little bitch Melanie. I wanted to scream at her, wanted to call her every nasty name I could think of. But I knew if I drew attention to myself, I wouldn't be able to pull off my next trick—escaping.

While the sergeant was still occupied with the other officer, I quickly made my way to the side door, opened it, and stepped outside. It was very dark out, but a fluorescent light illuminated the pathway to the sidewalk. Just as I prepared to take one step toward freedom, I felt a hand on my arm.

"And where do you think you're going?" asked the booming voice of Sarge. I spun around, and he began to walk me back inside. Still feeling all the anger brought on by the thought of my boyfriend screwing another woman, I attempted to wrestle myself away. Before I knew it, there were several cops grabbing me by my arms and legs. As I struggled to free myself from what seemed like five people manhandling me, I felt my shirt slip up over my head. Feeling the cool air of the police station on my half-undressed body jarred enough sense into me to allow myself to be subdued, and I landed in a small holding cell.

Inside the cell, I banged on the metal door and cried to be let out for the next hour. When I was finally able to calm myself down, the sergeant opened the door.

"I'm going to take you back to my desk, but you will not try to leave again, do you understand?" he asked.

I nodded. "Yes, I promise." I sat with the sergeant for the rest of the night, and as I sobered up I engaged with him on a variety of topics from working as a bartender to world peace. As the first glimmer of light began to shine through the rectangular window of the station door, I felt my eyes getting heavy with exhaustion. The phone on the sergeant's desk rang loudly, jolting me out of my stupor. He picked it up.

"Yep, still here. Okay, will do," he said into the receiver, before hanging it up.

I sat up straight in the chair, now feeling wide awake. "Am I going to be able to go home now?"

Sarge shook his head and explained I had committed a crime and would have to be locked up until I saw the judge or someone came to bail me out.

I hadn't paid much attention to him when I first arrived at the station, and now as he stood up to escort me to jail, I noticed how tall he was. He was not my type but a good-looking guy, and his face seemed kind of—gentle. He stared at me for a minute with a somewhat puzzled look. "You are not the same person who came in here last night," he told me. "You seem very bright. Why are you here? I really hope you can get on the right track, because it seems like it would be such a waste if you didn't."

I was placed in a detention area with many other women, most of whom looked to be very rough around the edges. While waiting for my mom to come bail me out, I found a seat next to a table where a young woman was sewing clothes on a little machine. I couldn't help but notice the track marks lining both of her arms.

"You making that for your baby?" another woman asked her.

The sewing lady held up a little dress. "Yep, I'm hoping for a girl this time."

I had never felt more out of place, and the sergeant's words echoed in my brain, "Why are you here?" *I have no fucking idea,* I thought. *But I never want to come back again.*

You may be surprised to find out that night *wasn't* my rock bottom. I still had a domestic violence assault charge to acquire and much more drinking and drugging to do. Although the sergeant's words were very impactful, it was a much lesser offense that started to turn me around.

I was twenty-seven years old and, after an eight-year-long string of bartending in various dives, had landed my first "respectable" job, as a checker in a grocery store. After a previous arrest, my parents had taken away the car they had been letting me use. This forced me to move into their house, half a mile from the grocery store, so I could walk to work. Then I promptly lost the job when I showed up to my graveyard shift drunk. After all the times I had been in trouble with the law, in drug- and alcohol-filled abusive relationships, and in the darkest of dark depression-filled days, this was finally my rock bottom. I just couldn't bear to look at my parents' faces one more time after yet another major downfall. It had to end.

The medical insurance from my grocery job was still available even though I had been fired, so I would be able to afford to go to a treatment center. Or so I thought. Then I sat with the intake person and learned my insurance only covered part of the program.

"Can you get your parents to cosign?" the counselor asked me.

"No!" I told her adamantly. "I just can't ask them for another thing." She told me it was okay, and they would work something out for me. They helped me to secure a loan with a repayment plan of one hundred dollars a month over the next three years. I often joked that making those payments were what kept me sober.

CHAPTER 7

THE LOVE OF A MOTHER FOR A SON

The family kitchen at the hospice care center was more than just a room. Soft light filtered through the window, inviting family members to rest on the cozy couches in the nook. A big pot of soup made from scratch and freshly baked warm cookies waited patiently on the counter to bring some level of comfort to grieving souls. This was a gathering place for the family members of our dying patients. It was where those whose hearts were breaking could commiserate.

On this day, as I walked in to snag one of those cookies, the grieving person I met there was Deborah, the mom of my young patient Robert. Robert had two kids and a wife named Nicole. To be perfectly frank, I wasn't a fan of Nicole. I found her to be overbearing, especially when I learned she had made the decision in what would now be her husband's final days to not allow his mom to see him anymore.

Prior to this awful decision, Deborah and I had chatted often and become somewhat bonded. We were the same age, both mothers to twenty-six-year-old men. The difference being that Keith was living in California, and Robert was unresponsive and dying of cancer. Now Deborah stood in front of me in disbelief, begging me to help her see her son, which was completely out of my hands. Nicole was Robert's legal spokesperson, and no one had the authority to override her decision, no matter how cruel it was.

"I'll talk to the doctor and social worker about setting up a care conference," I offered helplessly.

I didn't know what else to say. What could I say? Nothing. There were no words in the history of words that would take away this woman's pain. So, I said nothing else; I just reached out to her to offer a hug. She accepted, falling into my arms weeping, staining my brightly colored flowered scrub top, which, in its joyfulness, suddenly seemed out of place. The feelings I had for this woman, who was wracked by sobs, went beyond empathy. I could imagine how it would feel to be told I couldn't be with my dying son, and on top of that I would also have remorse for the years lost in our relationship due to my very poor life choices.

***

Once I stopped drinking and drugging, I started to become more interested in my son. After a while, with some convincing from my parents, Lenny started letting me see Keith every other weekend. Three years into my sobriety, I met my second husband, Joel, a Special Forces soldier. Being a military brat, I had grown up watching the John Wayne movie about this elite branch of the US Army. I was more than a little impressed by Joel's status as a Green Beret. Four months later, we were engaged, and soon after that, I was pregnant with my first daughter, Eden. Lenny trusted Joel, which meant he allowed me more visitation. Soon, Keith was spending most weekends and every summer with us.

When Keith was four years old, Lenny had remarried, and his new wife, Merris, had filled the mom role in his early years, providing love and support. But by the time Keith was twelve

and I was able to measure up to Merris in the mom department, he was ready to come live with us full time. A contributing factor to his decision was that, through Lenny and Merris's
union, Keith had gained a stepsister, who was the same age
as him.

To say there was some sibling rivalry would be an understatement. His sister bullied him relentlessly at home and
at school, where she recruited others to pick on him as well.
Keith was mild-mannered and didn't like conflict or confron-
tation. It was evident to me that he was miserable. I had so
much empathy for him, as I, too, had been the subject of such
abuse when I was a kid. When he told me he wanted to live
with me, I knew I owed it to him to advocate for that. I did not
hesitate to broach the subject with his dad.

Lenny's reaction was much more extreme than I expected.
I thought for sure he would have seen this coming—he had
to know how much Keith was suffering at his sister's hands,
right? Apparently, he was oblivious, because he was furious
with me for entertaining such a notion. He felt betrayed by
me, and worse, by his son. He threatened to revoke all visitation rights. Being the drugged-up druggie I had been when we
reached our custody agreement, I, stupidly, willingly signed it
without considering the statement "visitation as deemed appropriate by the father." This gave him the authority to exercise his threats against me, and I had no legal leg to stand on.
Seeing how distraught Keith was by Lenny's decision, Merris
stepped in and was able to convince him that Keith would
benefit from further reestablishing a connection with me. It
wasn't the first time Merris had intervened on Keith's behalf;
she was always his champion. I owe a lot to her.

We agreed on a plan for Keith to live with me for one year,
but it was delayed when Joel got a new work assignment and
we had to move to Okinawa, Japan. Lenny eventually relented
and said Keith could move in with us for our final year of being

stationed there. At the end of eighth grade, Keith stepped off the plane at the Naha Airport in Okinawa, as he had done on two visits before, but this time he was staying. The moment I saw Keith walk through the glass doors to the waiting area, I was simultaneously overwhelmed with happiness and relief. I burst into tears, knowing he wasn't going to be leaving at the end of the summer. He never went back to live with Lenny again.

***

Just as I had been granted a reprieve with my son, so had Deborah. It was seven thirty in the morning as I walked down the hall toward the nurses' station. My report with Carl, the night-shift nurse, would be starting soon, and he would fill me in on all the happenings from overnight. I glanced across the station and immediately noticed a closed door with a postcard taped to it. The picture on the card was a leaf with a dewdrop on it. We used these postcards often. Sometimes one could walk down the hallway and count three, four, or five of them on closed doors. They might have seemed insignificant; they were anything but. They signified that, though a patient was still present in the room, they were no longer living.

The room with the postcard was Robert's, and now I knew Robert had died. *Wow, I wasn't expecting that!* I thought.

"What happened?" I asked Carl. "He didn't look like he was going to go that fast." Carl was an intense guy, the type of person who stood way too close and stared directly into your eyes when speaking to you. He was also gay and a little dramatic, not to say one had to do with the other.

"Bleed-out," he said matter-of-factly. "The tumor in his neck eroded his carotid artery." He paused, I think waiting for a dramatic response to the dramatic news.

I obliged. "Oh my God," I gasped.

"It. Was. Awful." He emphasized each word. "Blood was spurting out all over the place." Now he was gesturing at his own neck with his hand, yet more theatrics. "It looked like a crime scene. Blood everywhere. I swear it shot six feet out from the bed." I got the picture.

I thought about Deborah, who had been banished from his room. Maybe that wasn't a bad thing after all. Of course, it did mean his very young wife would have witnessed the traumatic ending to her husband alone. "How did his wife handle it?" I asked.

"She wasn't with him; his mother was," he told me, this time without any dramatic flair, which surprised me because *that* fact was almost as shocking as the bleed-out. He further explained that our hospice doctor had met with Robert's wife in the afternoon to encourage her to change her mind. It worked. Our doctor was incredible at guiding people to the right choice, and Nicole had decided to let her mother-in-law visit. I was both relieved and horrified. Robert's mom was finally allowed to be with him, and then he bleeds out in her presence?

"That must have been horrible for her!" I was now delivering the drama response I think Carl had been expecting from this wild ride of a story.

Certain types of cancer can result in catastrophic bleeding. It isn't common, but we prepare for it just in case. There were dark sheets on the beds and dark towels in the "bleed-out kit" to minimize the appearance of the bright-red blood. The kit also held gowns, gloves, booties, and masks with face shields. Medication orders were at the ready for midazolam, a sedative to treat the anxiety or shortness of breath that can happen. However, people who have a catastrophic bleed-out don't often live long enough to get the meds.

"Deborah did okay. It went as well as it could have under the circumstances. The dark sheets did help a little," Carl said.

"I told her to hold his hand while I went and got the midazolam. When I came back to the room, he was gone." As overly theatrical as Carl could be, he exuded compassion. I knew his calm presence had probably made the situation much easier for Deborah.

Sometimes things seem to happen the way they're supposed to, and even though it wasn't optimal for a mother to see her child die in such a brutal way, she was probably better equipped to be there than his young wife. I was relieved about the change of heart by Nicole. I felt certain had she steadfastly prohibited her mother-in-law from seeing her child before he died, she would have later regretted it.

I suddenly remembered the postcard on the door. "Is he still in there?" I asked. *Is the room still bloody?* I wondered.

"Oh, no," Carl said quickly. "This all happened last evening. The mortuary already picked him up, and the room has been cleaned." He sauntered across the hall to the room. "I just forgot to take this off," he said, yanking the card off the door.

Always with the drama.

CHAPTER 8

RELIGION AND TRADITION

I see this sentiment often in my TikTok comment section:

> "I always open a window when someone dies."

> "What do you think about opening the window after they die?"

> "Do you open a window when your patient dies?"

No. I do not.

Something vitally important in end-of-life care is understanding culture and customs. Obviously dying people are a diverse group, because every person of every faith, ethnicity, and culture will eventually die. In hospice we should never proselytize. We aren't technically allowed to according to the Medicare regulations. Hospice care does include spiritual counselors (aka chaplains), and although the public often think these counselors are going to try to convert people, their actual purpose is for spiritual well-being. It's not religious unless that is what the patient wants. It is unethical to try to coerce a dying person into a belief—not to mention a waste of the precious little time they have left.

Assuming cultural practices falls under the same guise as proselytizing. End-of-life care is comfort-focused, but that doesn't just apply to physical symptoms. We need to meet people in their spiritual comfort zone as well.

Though I've read a few different explanations, I'm not exactly sure where the custom of opening a window after someone dies originated. But the intended purpose is clear in all versions: to let the spirit out. The problem is, like with any cultural practice or religion, not everyone believes in that, or if they do and it's not executed appropriately, it can cause undue distress.

This came to light for me early in my hospice nursing career when another nurse opened a window after a patient died. When the family, who had not been present for the death, arrived, they were extremely upset, because they felt the spirit had been allowed to leave before they got there. Personally, I don't understand how a spirit couldn't just whoosh out under the door or through a keyhole. Still, the message wasn't lost on me: be mindful of people's beliefs and practices. If we don't know, we should ask.

Sometimes asking the dying person or their family about a cultural practice can be enlightening not only to the hospice clinicians but also to that family. A great example of this was with a Chinese patient, Mr. Wong, who was first seen by a social worker and another nurse while I was on vacation. From their reports, I learned that the family wanted to transfer him to a nursing home for his death. I presumed this was because they believed it was bad luck for him to die in the home—something many cultures believe. An ambulance would be needed to transport Mr. Wong to his future residence due to his extremely frail condition, and the social worker explained to the family the possibility that he may not survive the trip.

Those of us who work in hospice understand that for most people, the holy grail of a good death is to die in their own home. Dying in the sterile environment of a brightly lit hospital room is the antithesis of a natural death. Dying alone in an ambulance seems unimaginably awful to most people. However, the discussion with the social worker did not change the family's minds. They adamantly maintained that he should not die in the home.

Mr. Wong was bedbound and sleeping when I met him. Rather I should say he was couchbound, as the living room couch was where he was residing. His wife shook him gently and he awoke easily and was able to converse. Even though Mr. and Mrs. Wong spoke some English, I used a Chinese interpreter. Important conversations go better when there are no language barriers. His terminal diagnosis was colon cancer that had spread to his liver. His skin was yellow with jaundice, and he was very thin save for his abdomen, which was huge with bloat due to a bowel obstruction. Despite his failing condition, he didn't have any symptoms that caused discomfort, such as nausea, trouble breathing, or any of the other things that can go along with his disease. After I examined him, Mrs. Wong asked me to step into the kitchen, where we spoke in hushed tones with help from the interpreter. She let me know her husband had told her he was going to die in five days. Knowing that, although death is unpredictable, patients often have more insight about their impending demise, I suggested we sit down to discuss the plan to move him to a nursing home as soon as possible.

Because we couldn't be certain how long Mr. Wong would live, I explained to his wife we needed to do advance planning. Nursing homes almost always have a waiting list, especially the good ones. We couldn't just wait until he was closer to death and then put him in an ambulance and hope for an available bed. We needed to make a final decision on a nursing home and choose a date when we would send Mr. Wong there. It was a Tuesday and given his fragile condition (and his self-prognostication), I didn't think it unreasonable that he might die in five days. We started talking about moving him on Friday.

Mrs. Wong had already been tasked to pick out a nursing home by the social worker, who provided her with a list of nice ones in the area during her visit earlier in the week. She had not made any calls yet, as she wanted her son to assist her with the selection. Conveniently, he lived in the house next door, and as it was close to his lunch break, she was able to call him while I was still there. Within a few minutes he arrived at the house.

"I'm Jimmy," he said as he extended his palm.

"Penny," I said, shaking his hand, "the hospice nurse." I motioned for him to take a seat. Jimmy was bilingual, so conversing with him didn't require use of the interpreter. I explained to him the same dilemma I had communicated to his mom earlier: it was imperative we not wait to transfer his dad to a nursing home.

Through the course of our conversation, I finally asked Jimmy to educate me about Chinese culture and tell me why they didn't want Mr. Wong to die at home. He couldn't answer; he didn't know either. He turned to his mom and spoke to her in Chinese. Then he turned back to me. "I asked her why she thought my father couldn't die at home," he said. He then explained his mother thought Jimmy and his siblings wouldn't want him to die in the family home. Jimmy said he had never thought about it before but didn't think it would be a bad thing if he did.

I asked if they knew what Mr. Wong wanted. They both just stared at me blankly. Jimmy finally admitted they hadn't asked. Like many people who are afraid to bring death up with their dying person, they had hesitated to broach the difficult subject. I pointed out that Mr. Wong obviously knows he is dying, because he told his wife it would happen in five days. I suggested we ask him for his wishes. They agreed. I asked if they would like to ask or if they wanted me to do it. They volunteered me.

I went into the living room with the interpreter and kneeled on the floor next to the couch. It had been long ingrained in me that when using an interpreter, you always speak directly to the person you are addressing and not the interpreter. I also knew the best way to communicate would be to keep it simple and avoid euphemisms for easier translation. I looked directly into my patient's eyes as I spoke.

"Mr. Wong, do you want to go to a nursing home to die or do you want to die here in your home with your family?"

He glanced at the interpreter and then at me as he spoke slowly in English. "In my home, with my family."

The decision was made. Mrs. Wong was very confident she would be able to take care of her husband with her children's help. Since her son lived right next door, she felt well supported. I would make daily visits to give them whatever instructions and education they needed. As it turned out, my patient wasn't quite accurate with his prediction. Two days later, I walked in to find him taking his last breaths. He died minutes after I arrived. His whole family was gathered in the living room around him: wife, son, daughter, and grandchildren.

His daughter looked at me tearfully. "Your timing was perfect," she said.

"*Your* timing was perfect," I replied, acknowledging the presence of Mr. Wong's whole family being by his side.

It's not just culture that influences people at the end of life; faith can play a huge role in the death-and-dying arena. For me personally, not adhering to any religion is a relief. I never have to worry about trying to get to heaven or avoiding hell, because I believe neither exists. I don't have to question God, because I don't believe in God. That is, I don't believe in God as an omnipotent being that can control our lives and deaths. If I did believe in a God who orchestrated everything that happens in the world, I would be tormented with the question of why every time I took care of a dying young person.

There have been times when religion was a part of my life. When I got older and moved past thinking I wanted to be a flying nun like Sister Bertrille—and the disappointment when I found out she couldn't—my interest in religion grew. I think my parents were agnostic, or atheists. I actually have no idea. My parents were supportive in that they allowed me to go to church with friends. They didn't try to influence me one way or another, although they did make it clear that they would not ever be going to any church. As an adult, I am eternally grateful I wasn't indoctrinated. I have crossed paths with so many people who grew up in a religion only to suffer spiritually due to the unattainably high standards. But as a tween, I made friends at school who told me about how "fun" church was, and I wanted to know more. So whenever I was invited, I would tag along to see what it was all about.

It just so happens that the first church I attended for my informal investigation was Catholic. I was about twelve years old, and I thought the rituals were pretty darn cool. However, I did feel a disconnect between the idea that my friend and I could go shoplifting on Saturday and she could be forgiven for it on Sunday just by confessing. I mean, it would be one thing if she confessed and never did it again, but this was an ongoing practice. It didn't seem to matter how many times it happened as long as you could get absolved by the priest. Catholicism wasn't the only religion I learned was steeped in hypocrisy. My Mormon girlfriends also did not abide by the ways they were taught. They drank caffeinated beverages, smoked cigarettes, and sometimes even had premarital sex. After exploring these and other religions, I was dissuaded from the whole notion of going to church.

All that being said, I fully acknowledge that faith can be helpful to people in life and in death. I know people who, like myself, struggled with addiction and were able to get out of it through their belief in the power of God. I've seen dying people take solace in believing their journey will land them in heaven. I've also seen when it can be unhelpful. Often, people who are faced with the end of life, whether a loved one's or their own, will question God.

For example, my husband's great-aunt was devoutly religious. Then at the end of her life, which happened to be spent in a hospice care center where I worked, she grew concerned with the length of time it was taking her to get to heaven. At ninety-something years old, she had grown weary of the waiting game and would anguish, "Oh Lord, why am I still here? Why have you forsaken me?" I'll tell you, it's not something I want to be wasting my breath on when my time comes.

Pamela was a professional dancer and a health nut. Her sister-in-law affectionately referred to her as the "garden girl" because she was a vegan. She had never smoked, only drank socially, and had no family history of cancer. Her only health issues were constipation, which she wrote off as insignificant and addressed by taking various herbal remedies, and blood in her stool, which she attributed to her constipation. She should have been more concerned. Healthy lifestyle notwithstanding, this woman had fallen victim to the ravages of colon cancer and was dying at the young age of forty-two. When she arrived at the care center, Shannon and the doctor went in to see her first. They came back with looks of disbelief on both of their faces.

"I have never seen anybody in so much pain," Shannon said, sounding astonished. The doctor proceeded to rattle off instructions for medications that would help to get Pamela's pain under control. We have many important purposes as hospice professionals, but our main goal is always to make our patients as comfortable as possible while allowing a natural death to occur.

Later that shift, I passed one of the aides in the hall. "Have you seen the patient in room one yet?" she inquired of me. "She's so yellow, she looks like a Simpson! Why is she that jaundiced?" I had also heard whispers from another aide comparing her to a cadaver.

I feel I must pause here and acknowledge these descriptions could be considered crude and appalling. I always like to keep things real, though, and this is an example of the dark places those of us who work in hospice sometimes go to cope with the constant barrage of death and dying. Sometimes "dehumanizing" the human—outside of their earshot, of course—is the only way we are able to disassociate enough to be able to provide compassionate care without losing our shit. At this care center, we were working twelve-hour days in a sullen environment and needed to laugh occasionally. For the weekend team, as we called ourselves, this was our philosophy. Fortunately, we all shared the same sometimes gritty and macabre wit. Those who weren't used to us could definitely be offended or shocked by our little snippets of humor.

I explained to the aide the cancer had metastasized to Pamela's liver and, no, I hadn't yet had reason to go in there. I tried to respect the patient's privacy whenever possible. I wanted to help as much as I could but wouldn't take any pleasure going into a room just to gawk at someone as if they were a sideshow freak. If I had a legitimate, nursing-related reason to go in room one, I wouldn't hesitate to enter. Otherwise, I left the patient and family alone.

Our little dancer had arrived in the morning. It wasn't until close to the end of my twelve-hour shift that I had cause to go in to meet her. I was walking by her room when my patient call pager began to vibrate in my pocket. I whipped it out and read it: someone in room one had pushed the call light. I took a moment to compose myself before going in. Descriptions like "cadaver" and "Simpson-yellow" jetted through my mind. I took a quick breath and walked into the dimly lit room.

The young woman lay on her side facing the door. To say she was emaciated would be an understatement—she was skeletal. The skin stretched tautly over her bones was tinted bright yellow. Her lips were drawn back, mouth open wide to expose perfect white teeth. Long bleached-blond hair hung limply on her pillow. Pale blue eyes were open wide, their whites now as yellow as the rest of her. Not only did she look like she was dead, but she also looked as if she had been that way for a while.

Though I was almost horrified by what I saw, the family, who were seated around the room, would not have known it by looking at my solemn, composed face. I leaned over her. "What can I do for you?" I asked. Unable to speak, she only let out a soft, painful moan.

"I think she could use a position change; it's been a while and she still doesn't look comfortable," her husband, seated at her side, told me.

"Sure," I replied. "I'll grab someone to help me move her." I opened the door to the room just as Shannon was coming in. I had forgotten to switch off the call light when I entered, leaving it to continue paging everyone. The woman's husband leaned over her, stroking her hair and nuzzling her cheek.

"These nice ladies are going to try to help you get more comfortable," he said softly. "So don't you give them a hard time," he teased. Gently he kissed her head. "I love you, my beautiful baby." I can keep my nurse's face through some pretty tough things, but it was difficult to hold back the tears that welled up in my eyes as I watched the love emanate from this man to his dying wife. Blind was he to his corpselike bride; she was his one and only.

Through the weekend, I had the pleasure of learning a little about Pamela's life. She came from a devout Catholic family and had long been a single parent to a seventeen-year-old girl. She had met her husband, Jack, at a PTA meeting for the school his son and her daughter both attended. Though they had only been together for three years, the couple shared a lifetime's worth of passion. After Pamela's diagnosis, Jack had taken leave from his job to be by her side, and they traveled and enjoyed their precious last moments together on Earth. Just six months prior to Pamela's admission to hospice, they had been married in Greece. She had already been dealing with the ravages of cancer for a year before that. Jack proudly showed me a picture of his lovely wife dancing before she became ill.

"Up until a couple of weeks ago," he told me, "she was still practicing her ballet exercises in the hospital, using the bed rail as a barre."

I learned Pamela had told her sister-in-law she was all right with dying. "I've raised my daughter into a young woman, I've married the man of my dreams, and I had the beautiful wedding I always wanted. If that is all there is, then I am okay with that."

The one thing lacking in Pamela's life was her parents' approval. Although they were present at the hospice center to visit their daughter in her last hours, they were not much comfort to her. The information we had been given was that when her father found out about the terminal diagnosis, he told her she must have done something terrible for God to punish her like that. Being steeped in the old-fashioned Catholic teachings made them see their daughter as a sinner for divorcing her first husband. They were also very disapproving of Jack and didn't think their daughter should have married him.

I went in to check on Pamela the next day and met her parents. Her father sat stoically in a chair near the window, reading the morning paper. Her mother hovered over the bed of her dying daughter.

"It's so hard to see her like this," she said to me. I agreed that I could only imagine what it would be like to lose my child. "Why did this happen to her? Why?" she questioned me. "No one in our family has had cancer, and she took good care of herself," she went on.

I searched for the right words to say to this mother. Words that would let her know that her daughter was good and didn't deserve what she thought of as a punishment from God.

"You know," I began, "I've seen a lot of young people come here with cancer, and the truth is, we just don't know why they get it. Sometimes, no matter how good you are to your body, something goes terribly wrong. At this point, we can't ask *why* anymore, we can only try to support Pamela and make her as comfortable as possible." I turned to leave the room, then turned back around and faced the grieving mother. "I just want to say that Pamela is a very lucky woman to have found such a wonderful, supportive husband as Jack. It is so obvious to those of us who have been taking care of her that he is deeply in love with her. Some people never get to know that kind of happiness."

I don't know if it did Pamela's mother any good to hear my words of wisdom, but I hoped she could find some solace in my message. I saw Pamela a few more times that day and never again after that. Thankfully, the relief of death soon came with her loving husband by her side. And I, at the age of forty-two and with a lifelong history of chronic constipation, went to have my first colonoscopy. Just in case.

CHAPTER 9

THE DIGNITY AND INDIGNITY OF DYING

I am often asked how I feel about medical aid in dying and euthanasia. Medical aid in dying, or MAiD, allows a person with a terminal prognosis to legally purchase and ingest medications that will end their life. Euthanasia is when a medical provider administers the medications that will cause death. At the time of this writing, MAiD is legal in only ten states and the District of Columbia. Euthanasia is not legal anywhere in the United States.

In Washington, where I live, the Death with Dignity Act went into effect in 2009. I had been a hospice nurse for three years when it went on the ballot, and I didn't hesitate to vote for it. Despite working for a Catholic organization at that time, which was vehemently opposed to "physician-assisted suicide," as they referred to it, my hospice colleagues and I discussed the proposed bill behind closed doors and in hushed tones. All of us agreed it should be legal. Those of us who see the indignities some diseases can cause understand there are things worse than death. Not only do I approve of MAiD, I also think it should be federally legal, more accessible, and more affordable. As far as euthanasia, well, at the time of this writing, abortion just became illegal in some states. With this major backstep in healthcare, I don't see something else that could be miscon-strued as murder happening anytime in the near future.

Before I go on, let's talk monikers. Hospice as an institu-tion doesn't care for the term "death with dignity." Most hos-pice professionals, including me, feel that dying and death while on hospice can be very dignified, especially for those who have accepted their impending death and planned for it. When I think of dignity while dying, a patient who immedi-ately comes to mind is a somewhat famous photographer who passed the time in her hospital bed at our hospice care center writing her own obituary.

"How does that sound?" she would ask me after reading an excerpt while I pushed medication into her IV. "I want people to know about my accomplishments, but I don't want to sound too, you know, arrogant." I would tell her it sounded perfect while in my mind I was fascinated by not only the life she led but how she embraced her death so matter-of-factly. And then there were those families that advocated for their person's dig-nity when they were unable to speak for themselves, such as my patient's sister who insisted she not be in diapers.

Now let me step up onto my soapbox as I discuss the more offensive label "physician-assisted suicide." As anyone in the legislation-for-MAiD arena will tell you, there is a definite dis-tinction between suicide and someone with a terminal condi-tion ending their own life legally and safely. When someone dies by suicide, they have a choice to live or die and they are choosing to die. Typically, they are struggling with mental health issues. People who end their life with MAiD, on the other hand, have terminal illnesses. They don't have a choice. They are dying. They just want to be able to take control over their own life and the end of it. According to the *Journal of the American Geriatrics Society*, in twenty-three years of data on MAiD, 8,451 patients received the prescription but only 5,329 used it. Sometimes just having the ability to check out if the going gets tough is all a dying person really wants. When someone dies using MAiD, the cause of death on the certificate is their terminal disease, not suicide. Also important to note is that death by MAiD does not invalidate life insurance policies. A significant drawback that can hinder those who are seeking this option is that, even where legal, it is often not affordable or accessible, due to the long waiting periods.

One of the basic philosophies of hospice is quality of life over quantity of life, and quality and dignity go hand in hand. Unfortunately, as much as we try to ensure both at the end of a person's life, sometimes it's just not possible. For one thing, these ideals mean different things to different people. I've cared for many people whose bodies have turned on them in the most unimaginable ways, robbing them of both quality and dignity. Some people are able to cope with the changes that come along with disfiguring diseases, like the lady I cared for whose nose was surgically removed.

In nursing school, we were taught about the "nurse's face." When confronted with foul odors, disgusting-looking wounds, or any other unpleasant medical issues, a nurse must always keep a straight face. The last thing a dying person, or for that matter anyone suffering from a medical condition, needs is to be made to feel they are repulsive. It requires both skill and talent to accomplish the nurse's face. When I met the lady with no nose, having been offered *zero* warning of that important fact, my nurse's face was called to task.

I sat in the break room with the nurse who was completing her night shift as she went through the list of patients and gave me the rundown. "Room eight is still the eighty-six-year-old man who fell off the ladder and had a massive brain bleed," she said. *I remember that one,* I thought. His son had told me they kept warning him not to go up and clean the gutters but, in the end, he admitted if he gets to live to be eighty-six and then falls off a ladder and dies, it wouldn't be that bad of an ending to a long life. After all, he had maintained his independence until the end and what took him out was what he wanted to do. "Room ten is the young man with head and neck cancer," she continued. *Twenty-eight years old . . . sad situation,* I thought. There seemed to be some friction between his wife and his mother. "And room eleven is a new admit, Millie James. She has nasopharyngeal cancer. No pain issues, lots of friends visiting," she said. But she omitted the aforementioned and crucial bit of information that caught me completely off guard. It was a damn good thing I was a master of the nurse's face!

Mrs. James's face looked perfectly normal other than the gaping hole smack dab in the middle of it, where I could see every bit of anatomy in her sinus passages. "Hi, Mrs. James. I'm Penny, your nurse. How are you doing today?" I said to her without so much as blinking an eye.

"Oh, you can call me Millie," she said cheerfully. "We're having a little party. Want to join us?" She giggled. Millie was holding court with a few other ladies who also seemed oblivious to Millie's missing nose. And I mean, why wouldn't they be? She was absolutely lovely, brimming with joy. She held a spoon in her hand and plunged it into a jar of something green, then pulled it out and spread it on a cracker. "You have to try this," she said to me, holding the cracker out. "It's jalapeño jelly and it is delicious!" I did try it, and she was right; it *was* delicious. For years after, I made my own jalapeño jelly and thought of her every time I ate some.

Apparently, Millie did have a prosthetic nose, but she found it uncomfortable and chose not to wear it. The appearance of her missing proboscis was only cosmetic, but its absence caused her physical issues. The sinuses, being exposed, were prone to drying out and had to be irrigated regularly. She didn't complain when we did this task, but it seemed like it would have to be a little uncomfortable to have saline solution blasted directly into the sinus passages with a syringe. This was also another opportunity for me to exercise my perfected nurse face, as it not only had a bit of a foul odor but I worried I would drown her! By her own admission, though, Millie's quality of life was good. As long as she could party with her friends, she was happy and mostly unaffected by the deformity her cancer had created. She did not let her lack of a nose define her.

For some people, though, the betrayal of their own body is unbearable. From the moment my mother-in-law from my second marriage, Rayna, found out the surgery required to address the cancer left her with a colostomy bag, her quality of life evaporated. A colostomy creates an opening in the abdomen, aptly called a stoma, that is created from the large intestine, out of which stool is excreted into a bag attached to the person's body. As I stood by her bedside days after her surgery, Rayna threw back the covers, exposing the stoma. "My quality of life is over," she anguished. Rayna had been a model when she was younger and prided herself on her appearance. Now here she was, waking up from surgery not only having just been given a life expectancy of three months or less, but also with what she considered to be the ugliest, most disgusting thing she could imagine happening to her once-beautiful body. Had our state's MAiD law been enacted when Rayna was dying, I feel certain it was something she would have explored as an option.

I have to say, I don't blame her. I don't think I'm particularly vain when it comes to my appearance, but there are some things that can happen to a human body I wouldn't want to endure, especially if they came with a limited life expectancy. I remember one man who had no butt as a result of his colorectal cancer. Literally . . . *no butt*! He didn't seem to mind it much, agreeably laying on his side, reading his crossword while I packed piles of gauze into the cavern that used to be his bum. Of course, he couldn't really see what it looked like back there, and his Dilaudid infusion kept him pain-free. I'm not so sure how I would feel about missing what was considered my best feature when I was younger! And there is a type of breast cancer that causes fungating tumors, named aptly because they look like fungus. The breast becomes hard and ulcerated, leaks fluid, smells awful, and is very painful. While everyone's experience and opinions are different, I have to be honest: if that happened to me . . . Check, please.

Not only physical malformations impact dignity but also psychological and mental changes. One patient I cared for was a successful businesswoman in her mid-fifties with breast cancer. Had she known the cancer would metastasize to her brain and cause her to one day smear poop on her face, she might have opted out of life on her own terms. Thankfully she was blissfully unaware of her actions as she painted on her brown "blush" and "eyeshadow." Her friends and family were understandably horrified by it, however.

Even the threat of a condition causing someone's personality to change can be enough to drive them toward MAiD. Will, for example, had liver cancer, and from the day I met him, he expressed he was not going to let his disease play all the way out.

I ambled my Prius up the narrow road, eyes peeled, looking for my new patient's house. I wasn't sure I would even be able to see it through the thick of trees lining the single-lane drive. Instead of the usual evergreens so prevalent in Washington, I was surrounded on all sides by deciduous trees, mostly cottonwoods. Being spring, they were fully leafed out, secluding the road ahead of me. It was a clear day, and the sun peeking through holes in the leafy canopy created an almost ethereal effect. As my climb up the driveway suddenly leveled off, the trees opened, and I spotted a little house to my right. It sat perched up on a bank above the end of the driveway. I pulled in between two cars parked in the front and shut off my engine. Getting up to the house required a bit of a hike up rugged-looking stairs, and when I reached the top, I was met by a tall man who looked to be in his late thirties or early forties. I set my bag down on the porch.

"Hi, I'm Penny with hospice," I told him, reaching out to shake his hand. "Are you Will?"

The man let go of my hand and held the door open wider, motioning for me to come inside. "I'm Mark," he told me. "Will is just through here." I picked up my bag and proceeded into the house.

The first room we walked into was the kitchen, which was illuminated by bright sunshine pouring through wall-to-wall windows. We exited the kitchen into the living room, where there were more big windows. "It's nice and bright in here," I said, complimenting the living space to start building rapport. I did genuinely love the ambiance. A swivel-type recliner in the corner of the room swung around. The seated man had a faintly yellow complexion that almost made him look camouflaged in the beige leather chair.

"We're big on natural light," he said with a weak smile. A round of introductions by Mark informed me this was Will, my patient. Will was in his early sixties, and as I mentioned, his terminal diagnosis was liver cancer—hepatocellular carcinoma, to be exact. Will was Mark's senior by more than twenty years, and they were married. I would later learn they had met when Mark was only twenty-two years old and had both fallen instantly in love. At first, neither of their families were thrilled by the union. Eventually, Mark's family came around, but Will was from a generation that had a very hard time accepting homosexuality, and he continued to be estranged from them, even now when he was dying.

Right at that first meeting, Will made no secret about the fact that he was planning to take advantage of MAiD and end his own life within the next month. He began telling me all about his plan. Without turning my head, I slid my eyes to the right, glancing at Mark, who was seated next to me on the couch. I was curious to see his reaction to Will's final wish. I expected to see disappointment or at least sadness, but Mark nodded his head in agreement as Will walked me through the plan.

"The next step is for me to see another doctor to make my second request," he told me. I knew working for a religious organization wouldn't allow me to offer advice or information, or to be present when a patient consumed the lethal meds, but we would not discharge patients from hospice if they wanted to end their own life through the legal process.

At that time, Washington state law required at least a fifteen-day waiting period between the first and second request for MAiD. The request could only be made by the terminally ill person, and they must be determined to be capable of making their own decisions by two physicians. Will had already made the first request and had just about a week left until his second doctor's appointment.

"Mark is completely supportive of my choice to do this," he told me as he concluded with an explanation of his reason for wanting to take the matter of his death into his own hands.

Mark got up and walked over to Will, putting a hand on his shoulder. "Yes," he said, looking down at Will, tears starting to well up in his eyes. "And I will be with you until the very end."

Will reached up and patted Mark's hand. "I know."

A week later I drove back to Will and Mark's house for my second visit. The weather was not quite as nice; it was downright shitty. Rain, rain, rain, typical for Seattle. Even with the lush green vegetation surrounding the driveway, the atmosphere was more gloomy than otherworldly this time. Looking back, it seems like the gloom should have hinted at what kind of a visit I would have with Will, as things had taken a turn for the worse.

Just like last time, Mark greeted me at the side door, but his demeanor had drastically changed. His appearance was a little alarming. His hair was unkempt, and he looked like he hadn't slept for days. "What's been going on?" I asked him as he led me into the house.

He sighed heavily. "He hasn't been himself at all since yesterday. He's very confused."

"Where is he now?" I asked.

"He's in his chair. Our friend Dan is with him," he replied.

"It's okay, Will. Sit back down," a male voice said loudly from the living room. Mark and I walked in to find Will attempting to stand, as a short, balding man was trying to get him to sit back in the chair. Unfortunately, just like my patient Margaret at the care center, Will was experiencing agitation caused by rising ammonia levels in his brain. I instructed Mark to get the package of medications commonly known as the comfort kit, which most hospices provide for emergency use at end of life. He handed the package to me, and I opened it, pulling out the lorazepam.

Also called Ativan, this medication is in the benzodiazepine class—the same class as a more easily recognizable medication: Valium. I was able to persuade Will to take the pill, and the three of us sat with him until he began to calm down. He wasn't completely confused—he did seem to recognize me—but I could see the writing on the wall. Things were likely going to escalate. I instructed Mark to give the lorazepam as often as needed to keep Will calm and left knowing his desire to end his own life would now likely be off the table.

I made daily visits after that, and as I suspected, Will continued to get more out of control. Mark was giving lorazepam around the clock, but the effect was no longer enough to keep him calm. Will was becoming a danger to himself as his risk of falling increased with his confusion. Mark wasn't doing well either. He had already resigned himself to the fact that Will would not be able to carry out MAiD as planned. "Will's biggest fear when he learned about the symptoms related to his disease was losing control of himself. This is *exactly* what he didn't want to have happen!" he said, exasperated. That would become a familiar mantra over the next few days as Will's agitation and Mark's frustration escalated.

I arranged to get Will admitted to an inpatient hospice care center and, although the room and the setting were beautiful, Mark could not be appeased. Will had wanted to die in their home. Day after day Mark reiterated, "This was *exactly* what he did *not* want to have happen." Eventually, we were able to get Will's symptoms managed, but it did require sedation with an infusion and IV push medications. Mark was still angling to get Will home, but I was concerned that in his current emotional state, Mark would not be able to manage the meds on his own.

"What about if I got my cousin to help?" he asked. "She's a licensed practical nurse."

I'm not going to lie, I was dumbfounded. "You have a nurse in the family who would be willing to come and do this?" I tried not to sound too incredulous or annoyed that this bit of game-changing information had been withheld from me.

"Yes," he told me. "I know she would do it."

So that afternoon we arranged for the medications to be delivered and Will to be transported back home. I met Sandy, Mark's cousin, at the house and gave her the rundown on the meds. I was so thankful she seemed not only willing but very competent to take care of Will in his final hours. He died that night.

Although Will was not able to end his own life on his own terms, he was at least able to die in his own home. The problem when MAiD is not legal or accessible for whatever reason is that sometimes people will take matters into their own hands. Over the years, I've known of patients who overdosed on their hospice-prescribed meds or shot themselves, and even one who hung himself in the hospital bathroom. Whether the person "successfully" dies or not, the outcome in cases like these is never good. Not for the friends, family, or medical professionals who are often traumatized by this shocking outcome, especially if they are the ones who find them. And if the person doesn't die from their attempts, the outcome is not good for them either. Fractured ribs from resuscitation efforts or being intubated on life support in the hospital are not a pleasant end to a life. In other words, there really are fates worse than death.

CHAPTER 10

HELP ME LEAVE MY HUSBAND

Moving to Okinawa with Joel was good for me—not at first, but eventually. When I arrived, I was five months into a complicated pregnancy. Mia, the name we had already chosen for our future daughter, was shown to have a cyst on her brain during a routine ultrasound. The doctor explained the cyst might just be a benign anomaly and could resolve on its own, or it might indicate a much more serious underlying condition that would end in a nonviable pregnancy. Either way, I needed ongoing testing to monitor the situation. These tests, I learned only after moving to the tropical Japanese island, would not be available at the small military hospital on Kadena Air Base. Instead, I had to go to the nearest major military hospital—in Hawaii. The situation was made even more challenging by Eden, who was an exuberant, mischievous little toddler.

We couldn't get into military housing right away, so Joel found us a little house in town. Almost immediately he left on a mission, leaving me alone in a foreign country, where I didn't speak the language, with serious medical issues, a toddler in the throes of her terrible twos, and the most unbearable climate I had ever encountered. To me, it constantly felt like a thousand degrees with a million percent humidity and no rain. I had also never really been into the military-wives scene, so I had zero friends. Great.

I was thrilled when I met a few other moms with young kids who heartily accepted me into their unofficial club. We passed the time without our husbands on play dates at the park, shopping, and swimming at the pool on base. I was happy to have found new friends, but truthfully, I never quite felt assimilated into the group. At thirty-four, I was much older than my twenty-something companions. And as much as I like drama (did I mention I used to be a crisis addict?), the schoolgirl brand of gossip they seemed to delight in wasn't a good fit for me.

The feeling of being an outsider was made worse one blazing hot day when we all met at the pool. We plopped our littles in the kiddie pool and pulled up lounge chairs from which we could keep watchful eyes on them. Suddenly one of the moms jumped up.

"There's poop in the pool!" she said loudly enough for us to hear but hushed enough to not draw attention to the intrusive little floater.

I looked at another mom with a quizzical look. She leaned over and whispered, "If the lifeguards see it, they will have to shut the pool down for cleaning." The mom who had sprung into action was now in the pool and deftly scooped the mini-Snickers-sized piece of fecal matter up in her hand, then rushed toward the bathroom. Meanwhile, the other moms stared intently at the pool, scouring it for the source, the poop perpetrator. It didn't take long. Suddenly—*bloop, bloop, bloop*—little turds started popping up in a circle around my smiling little girl.

The pool was promptly closed, and I was never invited to join the other moms again. I was so mortified by the situation, I didn't even want to go there by myself and risk bumping into them. Without that reprieve to beat the heat as I grew steadily larger, I felt like I was in literal hell. But the situation improved greatly when Keith came to visit for his summer vacation. We retreated to the master bedroom, I cranked up the AC, and night after night Keith and I stayed up until the wee hours playing a computer game called Squarez while Eden lay on the bed watching *The Lion King*, or "Yion King," as she called it. We would sleep in late, get up, get dressed, eat a cold breakfast, and spend the day at the pool—a different pool from the one that bore the shameful history of Eden's accident. After we got home, still wet from swimming, we would stand in front of the fans to cool down. Then we'd eat a cold dinner, retire to my room, and repeat the cycle.

It was so helpful to have Keith there, plus I just loved having him around. He was twelve years old, babysitting age, and I could leave him with Eden when I went to my prenatal appointments, which (thankfully) all ended up being on island. As it turned out, the cyst on Mia's brain resolved and I didn't have to medevac anywhere.

I wouldn't say Keith was irresponsible, but he wasn't the best babysitter. Eden had been potty training, so I generally left her in cloth underwear. Once, I returned home after being gone two hours and Keith informed me the minute I walked through the door that Eden had pooped. As she toddled around the living room, I could see she still had a load in her pants.

"You didn't clean her up?!" I asked Keith.

He shrugged his shoulders. "I didn't know how. I just told her not to sit down," he replied as if that had been a perfectly reasonable intervention. I spent a good twenty minutes scraping dried poo off my child's bottom.

Overall, we did have some interesting and fun times that summer. We bought a book about all of the parks in Okinawa and made it our mission to go to every one of them. We didn't usually stay very long, because the heat was so unbearable.

Keith and I still look back at that time with fond memories, though it was certainly a "best of times, worst of times" situation. By the end of summer, Joel came home, Keith left, my parents came to visit, Mia was born healthy, and we were finally approved for military housing.

Life improved immediately after we moved to Camp Foster. We had central air conditioning and my neighbors spoke English. I had learned some conversational Japanese when we lived off base, but it was nice to be able to converse in my mother tongue. I enjoyed the shopping, the food, and the customs. Before we'd left Washington, I had started taking ice skating lessons, and was thrilled when they opened a rink nearby. I took up pottery lessons, too, and eventually even taught classes and sold my wares at craft fairs. I loved being a mom to my daughters and to Keith every summer when he came to visit.

Something else changed during my time in Okinawa—I started drinking again. From the beginning of our marriage, Joel had questioned my alcoholism. "How can you say you're an alcoholic when you don't drink alcohol?" he would ask me. The more he said it, the more I also wondered if I would be able to control my ability to drink. After all, I had become a more responsible parent and had a pretty good handle on this adulting thing. I found it easy to compare my previous life with my current one and was convinced I wasn't remotely close to being that partying trainwreck anymore. I could no longer fathom identifying with that person.

One day while at the pool, I met a woman who was a substance abuse counselor (this was before the more PC term "substance misuse"). I talked to her about my own drinking issues and how I had started wondering if my issues had more to do with my youth rather than true alcoholism. She told me things had changed in the arena of treating alcoholism and the new model was to approach it with moderation instead of abstinence. According to her, alcoholics in Europe who were treated with this method had a much higher success rate. It gave me food for thought, and I wondered if moderation would work for me. The next day I picked up the new copy of *Time* magazine and discovered an article all about this same shift of treatment approach the counselor had told me about. Coincidence or dumb luck, it seemed like destiny to me (as if destiny would ever include imbibing in alcohol!), and throwing away the eight years of sobriety under my belt, I started drinking again.

My foray back into alcohol started with a beer at an Okinawan resort Joel and I had taken the kids to for a little vacation. Though in my younger years I had been skilled at shotgunning beer, proudly defeating marines and sailors and impressing them with my chugging skills, I had never really cared for it much. Having now made the decision that I wanted to drink responsibly, not having methods of drinking to bypass my tastebuds limited how much I could tolerate. So I considered it a worthy beverage, as I was able to control my drinking for the most part.

After we did our three-year tour on Okinawa, the five of us boarded a Freedom Bird, or military-contracted commercial plane, and headed back to Washington. I had become very good at budgeting, and by the time we made this move, we had saved up enough to buy our first house. From the outside, it probably looked like we were living the American Dream. And for the most part, life was pretty good.

But Joel and I were nine years into our marriage and had been living back in the States for a few years when one day we decided to get divorced. That makes it sound a little uneventful, and it kind of was. Well, that is to say it was uneventful because we mutually agreed on the decision. With his military career having him away from home so often, I'd learned how to be independent and no longer felt the need to have a man in my life to complete me, as historically had been my MO. Throughout my life, my self-worth had always hinged on having a boyfriend or a husband. Sometimes even at the risk of emotional and physical damage.

Joel was never abusive to me, but our marriage had morphed into more of a sibling-like relationship than a loving, husband-wife partnership, and we bickered constantly. Although I had so far been able to drink only socially and without significant impact on my life, adding alcohol to our floundering marriage didn't improve things. Our disagreements were almost always over something little and stupid. The bickering became more frequent and eventually turned into heated arguments.

I had been contemplating life without Joel for a while, and I told my sister I was just biding my time until the kids were grown. "Penny," she said, "have you ever considered that Joel might decide to leave *you*?" I had not. Even though I did feel I had grown to a level of independence that would allow me to survive without a man, I didn't want to find myself single-parenting without a backup plan. She encouraged me to start taking one college class a quarter, reminding me she had just recently earned a BA after ten years of doing just that.

A week later, Joel and I were getting ready for bed when I broached the subject of school. He immediately shot me down, suggesting instead we should invest our money into property. As usual, a major blowout ensued. But this time, it didn't follow the usual course of dragging on endlessly, with us both vying to be right. It ended when we literally both threw our hands up in the air, plopped down on our bed, and said in unison, "Let's get a divorce!"

Of course, in hindsight, I won that argument, because ironically the decision made school become a necessity and not something he would still be able to consider frivolous. If I didn't go to school, no job. If I didn't have a job, we would both be doomed to stay in a situation that was far from domestic bliss.

Joel's military income had allowed me to be a stay-at-home mom. I had even been homeschooling the girls, who were now six and eight years old. Other than the pottery instruction and a part-time job as an ice-skating-rink attendant, I hadn't really worked during our marriage. We both knew that lifestyle wouldn't be sustainable once we divorced. Investing in myself and my future career was the only way to ensure a successful divorce.

I picked up the newspaper and started to peruse the classifieds, noticing there were a *lot* of nursing jobs. *I could be a nurse,* I thought. Once upon a time, years ago, I had been a vet tech, and I was good at it. *There probably isn't much difference between nursing animals and nursing humans,* I surmised. So, nursing school it would be.

One of the things Joel and I had done right during our marriage was to purchase a large house. The split-level design had a full suite downstairs, and that, along with Joel's military career offering him extended absences during the transition, allowed us the luxury of being separated without full-on separation of dwellings. Still, neither of us was thrilled about living in the same house forever, so I decided to expedite my nursing career by first becoming a licensed practical nurse, or LPN, which was only a yearlong program. There were prerequisites required, though, and I had zero college under my belt. So I spent the next few months getting those accomplished before I was nursing-school-ready.

Although enlisted military pay is a reliable source of income, it doesn't make one rich, especially in a single-income household. However, it apparently deems one rich enough to not qualify for financial aid. I tightened up expenses as much as we could reasonably afford to, but with books and tuition, it would be a stretch to make work. Then one day I was listening to the radio and heard about a woman who had created Save Karyn, a website asking people for money to help her pay off her credit-card debt. And it was working! People were sending her money. Well, I thought if people will pay for some chick's extravagant purchases, maybe they would help me with my schooling. After all, becoming a nurse was a much nobler cause than supporting a shopaholic! And so HelpMeLeaveMyHusband.com was born (side note: it no longer exists, so don't bother going to the URL).

My website launched in 2002, when crowdfunding wasn't even a twinkle in the internet's eye. I had no idea how controversial my venture would become. The home page told a blameless story of how our lives had grown apart and we wanted to get divorced but needed help with funding for my college. I also blogged about my day-to-day activities, how I was managing school and parenting the kids, and tips for saving money. I had a mailbag where people could write in and I'd respond, mostly in a humorous or sarcastic manner because there were some haters hating.

> To: Penny
> From: Mark
> you sound very selfish i wouldnt give you shit

> To: Mark
> From: Penny
> Well, Mark, if I was asking for donations of fecal matter, this would be very discouraging.

> To: Penny
> From: Herbert

Why should I help you pay for your stupid mistake. Everybody wants a free hand-
out. You couldn't be dumber if you cut your
head off.

From: Penny
To: Herbert
I don't know, Herbert. Cutting my head
off seems like a pretty stupid thing to do.

Since my ultimate goal was to raise money, I included the information for my PayPal account and PO box, where I instructed people who found my site entertaining that they could send "a buck or two." In the very beginning, the website had little traffic. That changed rather quickly when a local television station reached out and was looking to do a human-interest story. People had been looking for a reprieve from the yearlong barrage of tragic news in the wake of the 9/11 bombing of the World Trade Center. So, when they got an anonymous tip about my website, they thought it would be a nice change.

Okay, the tip wasn't exactly anonymous. The tip was from me, I was the tipper. If I'm writing a book to tell my truths, I might as well be *wholly* truthful. The news station reached out because I sent them an anonymous email complaining about "some woman on the internet begging for money so she can divorce her husband." Any publicity is good publicity, isn't that the saying? Joel was deployed on some Special Forces secret mission, and I didn't know if he had internet access. I hadn't told him about the website because I was concerned the image on the front page of the site, a picture of me facing away from the camera, hands tied behind my back, would make him think I was saying derogatory things about him (though I never did).

I did an interview with the local news incognito, using my maiden name and hiding in shadows.

Although the horrific shock of 9/11 and the aftermath had flooded the media in the year before all this, there wasn't much going on in the world when the story aired. Because of that, the Associated Press picked it up, and overnight my website was flooded with emails. This included many requests for radio interviews from stations across the continents. I spent my mornings getting up early to talk with DJs in the United States, England, Ireland, and Australia. People in the United Kingdom were especially fascinated with this "American woman who was asking strangers to help pay for her divorce." Although asking for money for flats (what they call apartments) over there was commonplace, this was pretty much unheard of for someone from our country. The response in my homeland was more mixed; I had many supporters overall, but there were some assholes too. It didn't help that the press referred to this method of asking for help as "internet panhandling." Remember, this was way before the birth of social media and, more significantly, GoFundMe.

Once I broke the news to Joel, and after he got over his initial anger and realized I was earning money, he said he was okay with me showing my face to the public. This opened up possibilities for me to do television interviews and show myself in all my glory: no more anonymous shadowed woman with a robot voice here! I was interviewed on several local and national shows. I was flown to Los Angeles, where I was on a show called *The Other Half*, hosted by Mario Lopez and Danny Bonaduce, among others. As a diehard fan of *The Partridge Family*, meeting Danny was a big deal. The interview was fun, and Danny even pledged five dollars, though he never did pay up.

The pinnacle of my fifteen minutes of fame was when I was interviewed on *The View*. The interview itself was kind of lame.

Barbara Walters wasn't there that day, and other than Lisa Ling, who was very sweet, I found the hosts to be self-involved, more interested in spouting performative sound bites than actually learning about me. But the coolest thing that happened, one of the coolest things in my whole life, I have to say, was meeting the actress Geena Davis. After the interview, I walked backstage to where a crowd of people stood.

"She was very good," I heard a familiar voice say. "Very articulate." The crowd parted, and this towering, gorgeous goddess who was *the* Geena Davis walked toward me with her hand extended. "Hi, I'm Geena."

I shook her hand and stammered out words I feel embarrassed about to this day, "I loved *Beetlejuice.*" Geena Davis was an Oscar-winning actress, and it sure the fuck wasn't for *Beetlejuice*! Still, this is a memorable moment I will damn sure have in my obituary someday, "Geena Davis called me articulate."

CHAPTER 11

A HOSPICE NURSE IS BORN

I completed my nursing prerequisites as summer ended and started nursing school right away that fall. I was surprised, and relieved, to find out I wasn't the oldest student in the classroom as there were two other people clearly older than I was. I was scanning the room for a place to sit when I heard a familiar voice from behind me, "Hi, Penny!" It was Anna, the wife of one of the Special Forces soldiers on Joel's team. Despite an age difference of ten years, me being the senior, Anna and I became fast friends. At first, it was great to have a study buddy, but halfway into the school year, our friendship disintegrated. If I felt I had contributed to the dissolution in any way, I would be honest, but that wasn't the case. It seemed college was as cliquey as high school, and when Anna found someone closer to her age, she moved on. "I don't *not* want to study with you anymore," she told me when I asked why she kept turning down my requests to get together. *What the hell does that even mean?* I thought. As it turned out, she must have just inserted an extra "not" in there, because the friendship was over.

After that disappointment, I kept to myself. I was too busy taking care of my kids and studying to get embroiled in another drama. I was also very occupied with my website, which was now taking up a significant amount of time with the TV and radio interviews.

Just as opinions about my website within the nation were mixed, so were they in my nursing program. At first, my classmates didn't know about it, but once I ended up on national television, it became the water-cooler topic du jour. I often heard the *psspsspss* of whispers of disapproval behind my back. But I had bigger worries than how a few youngsters felt about my internet success. One day my teacher called me into the office.

"We got your background check from the state patrol," she said, holding out a piece of paper. "What can you tell me about this?" She tapped her finger on the words "assault 4." I knew it was most likely about an altercation with an abusive boyfriend that had landed us both in jail and apparently resulted in an assault 4 charge on my record. I say "apparently" because it had been fourteen years since the incident, and I only vaguely remembered the outcome. I did—and still do—remember the event, though. It's pretty much seared into my brain.

This was after the car accident where the two men who'd abducted me claimed I'd been driving and I'd wound up in jail. My parents had bought me a car to use, but after that, they felt I couldn't be trusted, so they took it away. One night, I convinced my best friend, Debbie, to take me to a club where I knew Mitch would be. Remember the abusive loser I pined for that awful night in jail? I suspected he would be with the bitch he had cheated on me with, but I didn't tell Debbie that. I didn't even tell her I knew Mitch would be there. Debbie had been one of my closest friends for years, one of my few "normal" (read: not alcoholic or druggie) friends, and she had warned me away from him over and over. She would not have taken me out that night if she'd known. I just told her I wanted to go dancing and that I knew of a great club.

I spotted Mitch immediately after we walked in, and of

course, he was with her. I wasn't drunk or even buzzed—I hadn't even had one sip of alcohol yet, so I'm not sure how my rage escalated so quickly. What happened next was another one of those "not my finest moments" situations. I started screaming at her, "Did he tell you I have herpes?!" In my infuriated state, I wasn't thinking about how self-deprecating the statement was; I just figured it would be enough to scare her away from "my man." And, incidentally, it was true. I contracted herpes when I was twenty, after having slept with just three men. Back in the eighties, that was a big deal you never told anyone about (well, except for your partner, if you had any integrity). These days, a lot of adults I know have it and are perfectly capable of managing symptoms. Anyway, Mitch was understandably humiliated and got up to leave.

I followed him to the parking lot, where my rage continued. We screamed at each other until our match turned into a physical fight, ending with me on the ground and him on top of me. I heard loud footsteps running toward us, and the next thing I knew he was being swept off me. "It's about time, you son of a bitch!" I screamed at him as a cop slapped handcuffs on him. Then I got the bad news as another cop apologetically explained that Washington state law required both parties in a domestic dispute to be arrested.

Now, all these years later, sitting in front of my teacher with my future in the balance, I fought back tears. I clutched my hands tightly over my stomach to quell the sick feeling that had come over me as I told her the story. Well, not all of it—I chose to omit the embarrassing detail about my very public STD proclamation. Relief came when she explained it would not preclude me from getting my nursing license. *Wow, it would have been nice if she had opened with that!*

As the year of the program was winding down, one of my classmates approached me. "I feel like I should ask for your autograph," he said as he held out a copy of *Time* magazine. I had already known about the article featuring my website when a friend excitedly called me with the news. He offered to pick up a copy of the publication for me, which I politely declined. I was starting to feel so over the whole thing by then. He laughed. "Did you ever think you would someday be mentioned in *Time* magazine—*TIME* MAGAZINE—and not even want to keep a copy of it?" I had to admit I didn't.

In the end, the website was more of a motivator than a real money maker. I did earn a little more than two grand, but more importantly, I received many emails and snail-mail letters of encouragement. The accountability of having a website with worldwide attention forced me to succeed. Disclosing your plans in public, whatever they are, can be a powerful motivator for success. Many years later, I would find the same accountability and motivation when I announced my second attempt at sobriety to over a hundred thousand TikTok followers.

I graduated from my program and decided to take the first nursing job I could get. Other students in my class had warned against going to a medical clinic (as opposed to a hospital), where one would "lose their skills." *As if they are experts,* I scoffed internally. By the time I graduated, I had put a Foley catheter in a dummy and given a shot to an orange. I hadn't done anything on a real live patient and didn't feel I had any skills to lose at that point.

As it turned out, working in the clinic gave me great experience, and I actually was able to develop some valuable skills and knowledge. I learned the art of a great nursing assessment, how to read and interpret lab values, and all kinds of important information about medications. I also had an impressionable encounter with a hospice nurse, who called to ask for a continuation of hospice for one of our patients.

"What do I need to do?" I asked her.

"I tell you the patient still qualifies for hospice, and you say, 'Yes, the doctor approves,'" she explained. "This call is just a formality. The patient really is dying and still qualifies." She had such an air of confidence that I found myself impressed once again by the specialty of hospice nursing.

I had been infatuated with the amazing, compassionate hospice nurses who cared for Rayna when she was dying of cancer. I recognized the work they did as sacred. Even though I had turned my treacherous life around and become a better mother, daughter, sister, and human, I still carried the burden of all the bullshit I had put my family, friends, and even total strangers through, from abandoning my son to lying to my parents to once even slapping a waitress in my drunken stupor when she tried to cut me off. I felt the need to make up for the red in my spiritual ledger. I wanted to be of service to people in a way that could really make a difference in their lives, and hospice fit the bill.

Admittedly, I also had a morbid curiosity about death. At the age of forty-one, I had never seen a real live—well, real dead, I guess—deceased person. After suffering from death anxiety (more on that later) for over a decade, I thought being around dying and dead people could help. Like exposure therapy, it might desensitize me enough to allow me to get over my fear.

So, after working a year in the clinic, with my eye on the endgame of being a hospice nurse, I decided to go work at a hospital, where I could learn more of the skills my fellow students had been so worried about losing. Unfortunately, that job was short-lived. Hospitals apparently often underwent a cycle of laying LPNs off about every ten years, and they had just hit the target. After only three months, I found myself needing another job.

I had seen a hospice care center being built three blocks from the home of my new boyfriend, Randy, whom I had begun to date during nursing school. (Spoiler alert: he's my husband now!) "Someday, I am going to be an RN and I am going to work there," I would tell him whenever we passed by the small, unassuming structure that looked more like a house than a medical facility.

For some reason, I was under the impression that LPNs were not able to work in hospice, which is why I thought I would need to be a registered nurse. However, there I was about to be unemployed, and I decided, *What the heck, I may as well check in on it.* It felt like the hospice care center had a neon sign above it flashing, "Penny, your dream is within your reach." Lo and behold, the care center was preparing to open its doors in just a few weeks and they were short exactly one LPN. They offered me the position during my interview.

I don't think I would be half the hospice nurse I've become if it wasn't for Shannon, the amazing mentor I had at that care center, this woman who taught me everything. Shannon was ten years my senior, with curly blond hair topping her svelte six-foot frame and a gentle yet commanding demeanor that reminded me of a warrior princess. A former ICU nurse, she had worked in hospice for six years, and as far as I was concerned, she knew everything there was to know about taking care of dying people. Later, I would tell people Shannon deserves most of the credit for my success as a hospice nurse. She was graciously willing to impart all her wisdom to me, and I absorbed it like a sponge.

For example, Shannon taught me the importance of managing constipation and how to disimpact patients, which is the clinical way of saying removing poop from someone else's anus with your own gloved fingers. It's not a fun task, but it is imperative to keep dying people from being uncomfortable and getting agitated. One time I plopped down in the chair at the nurses' station and noticed a brown smear on my scrub pants. *I don't remember eating any chocolate,* I thought. Then

I realized I hadn't. But what I had done was disimpact the guy in room nineteen an hour ago! Ewwww! But Shannon and I laughed about it for hours. It's a toss-up for me over what was worse: that, or the time I dumped a big poop from a bedside commode bucket and the toilet water splashed up into my face.

Shannon showed me tricks for putting catheters in men with enlarged prostates, how to access an implanted port, and how to be calm in the presence of drama, as with our poor lady who'd chucked the coffee cup at her. She knew everything there was to know about all the hospice meds, and I would listen in awe as she rattled off suggested orders to the docs. *Someday,* I thought, *I will be able to do that too.* And eventually, I was.

Whether it related to dealing with people's shit—literally and metaphorically, because, wow, emotionally stressful situations can bring out the worst in people—or it was valuable education in managing pain symptoms, I learned to be a great hospice nurse under Shannon's tutelage. She made working in what many people assume is a sad environment not sad and sometimes even fun. She and I also shared the same humor, which was often dark.

One evening I stood next to her as she received a call about a late admission we were expecting. "Oh, he died?" I heard her say. "Okay, thank you." She hung up the phone. "No admit," she said, reaching up to slap my hand in a high-five. Later, when I told my husband about it, he said he couldn't believe we high-fived over someone dying. I mean, it wasn't like we caused it or anything. We were just happy not to have to work overtime.

This was another truth I learned from Shannon. When caring for the dying, maintaining some modicum of levity is imperative to good mental health. Although it is both humbling and rewarding to have the honor of guiding people on this once-in-a-lifetime journey, working in hospice can devastate you if you let it. Burnout, compassion fatigue, and secondary trauma are just some of the symptoms all people in this line of work face.

What working in hospice didn't do was make my death anxiety worse. Instead, as I had hoped, it made it better.

CHAPTER 12

ACCEPTING THE UNACCEPTABLE

You've been told your person is dying. What next? Or worse, you've been told *you* are dying, which, don't lie, you know is worse, because most of us want to think about our own mortality even less than the mortality of others. But the reality is that thinking about our inevitable demise, accepting it, and planning for it are the best ways to have a good death.

Okay, now you want to ask, But what does that mean? What is a good death? It is whatever you envision for yourself. That might be a dark room filled with chamber music and being surrounded by a few solemn people, or a party atmosphere with raucous laughter and reminiscing. You might want to try to grin and bear the pain, or you might want to be nine sheets to the wind with as much pain medication as is legally able to be prescribed. You might be content with going to sleep and drifting away into oblivion, or you might envision fighting until your last breath to hang on (which will only work until it doesn't work). Whatever you or your person's plan may be, the important thing is to plan for it. And that starts with accepting that it really is going to happen.

Although we don't like to talk about death in our society, we all secretly think about it, some people more than others.

No matter how much someone is accepting of death and our inevitable end theoretically, it is normal to be scared when a terminal diagnosis hits. It's also normal for their friends, family, and anyone else who encounters a scared, dying person to feel helpless and want to do something to remove their fear. On social media, when someone wants to call your attention to a specific video, they can tag you by your username so you get a notification. I've been tagged in countless videos where someone has just heard they or their person is dying, and they are scared or crying. "@hospicenursepenny HELP THEM," they will write in the comments. My response is always the same: I can't. When a person is told the end of their life is closing in on them, they need time to process the information.

Of course, they may be sad and, of course, they may be scared. That is normal. It's human nature to want to survive. When they are finally able to embrace the life they have left rather than lament the life they won't have, it can be a beautiful thing.

Jessica was a young woman with colon cancer sharing her journey on TikTok. When she found out she had the short life expectancy that qualified her for hospice, she was terrified, and she made a video sharing her tears and worries. That video received over ten million views, and I was tagged hundreds of times. My response was to make a video letting people know it was normal and okay that she felt that way. Once she had a few days to digest the news, Jessica started posting videos about achieving her bucket list. I, along with some other creators, shared her videos, and soon she was receiving care packages from people all over the country. One of her last wishes was to try beignets—deep-fried pastries that are covered in powdered sugar.

There happened to be a young man on TikTok who had a beignet food truck. Through crowdfunding, he was able to fly across the country to make beignets for Jessica and her family at a Mardi Gras–style celebration. It was a beautiful journey to watch unfold on social media, and a testament to how much quality of life can be improved at the end once people reach that place of acceptance. And that quality doesn't have to include huge social media success, or even achieving your bucket-list items. It can simply be focusing on the present and the people, pets, and things important to you.

Death is so often the elephant in the room. Everyone knows it's going to happen, but no one wants to talk about it. When I come into homes to care for dying people, I am often asked by family members not to say I am with hospice. They say they don't want to stress the person out, cause them to give up hope, make them die faster, yada, yada, yada. I can confidently speak for all hospice nurses when I tell you this is one of the worst requests we get.

By the way, it also goes against the Medicare hospice regulations. The hospice benefit is elected, and they must be told they are electing it if they have the ability to comprehend what that means. If someone doesn't understand what it means, we can honor that, especially if being told they are dying over and over is traumatic for them. But don't ask us not to tell a person who has the capacity to understand that they are dying. It isn't fair to us, and it is most assuredly not fair to them. Will they be scared or upset? Probably, but they have the right to know so they can determine how they want their ending to look and to grieve their own impending death. Also, I believe people know they're dying even if they don't want to admit it or are in a little denial. The famous hospice nurse and author Barbara Karnes says, "We live in our bodies, we know when we're dying." That makes sense too. Think about anytime you've ever been sick— you know it!

Accepting the terminal diagnosis is just the tip of the iceberg, because there are many more decisions to make, and the best person to make them is the person whose life will be coming to an end. Unfortunately, many times the dying person will consider their family's feelings in that decision-making process and may feel the need to try everything to live as long as possible. But they often do this solely for their loved ones and end up living far past when they are ready to be done with the poking and prodding and waiting endlessly in clinics, hospitals, and emergency rooms.

I get asked all the time if I am afraid to die, and the answer is no. Am I excited about it? Also no. But I'm for sure not scared. However, that is easy for me to say—I'm fairly healthy. I'm not a patient sitting in a doctor's office, being told I have a finite amount of time left. If I was, I would probably be shitting my pants. But as I've said, there was a time when I was death obsessed. Death anxiety is a fear of death that involves overwhelming and extreme feelings of dread and distress when thinking about one's own death or the deaths of others in a way that interferes with daily life. It's persistent and pervasive, and I believe it's a direct result of our cultural failure to talk openly and honestly about death, especially to children.

I was nine years old when I had my first exposure to death. "Grandpa died," my mom told me and my sister. My brother was only four and was excluded from the conversation.

"What does that mean?" one of us asked. I don't remember which.

"It's like he went to sleep, but he won't wake up," she told us.

WHAT THE FUCK?? I thought. All right, I'm pretty sure the F-word wasn't yet a part of my vocabulary, but that sentiment was there. My paternal grandfather had lived in Manitoba, Canada, and I had met him just once, so I wasn't particularly emotionally invested in his life or death. However, the news that a person could simply go to sleep and never wake up again was horrifying.

One night soon after, I wandered into the living room where my mom sat watching TV. "Mom? I can't fall asleep," I said meekly.

"Why can't you sleep?" she said, slightly irritated. My dad was deployed with the navy, leaving her to be tasked with all the fun questions.

I swallowed hard. *Do I tell her? Do I say the word? If I say it, will that cause it to happen?* "I just keep thinking—what if you die?" I finally blurted out.

"Well, stop thinking about it," she said, now more than slightly irritated. "Think about something nice instead, like flowers."

I walked slowly back to my room and then appeared before her again just a short time later. "When I think about flowers, I think about cemeteries," I wailed, "and when I think about cemeteries, I think about you *dying*!" For the life of me I can't remember where the conversation went from there. My mom truly is a compassionate and loving person, though she was obviously misguided in how to approach conversations around death. In her defense, adults feel uncomfortable talking to other adults about death let alone talking to children about it. This was true back then and still is to this day! To her credit, she did use the actual word "died" when she told us about our grandpa, so kudos to her for that. Many people who are uncomfortable with the topic opt for euphemistic language, like "passed away," "in a better place," or "resting in peace," but in my experience, that doesn't help anyone, especially children.

When I became a hospice nurse, I hoped the exposure through my work with the dying would alleviate my death anxiety, and as I said, it did. Learning about and seeing the dying process, especially those deathbed visions, gave me more perspective on what it actually meant to die. Soon I was talking about it to my colleagues, my patients and their families, and my own family and friends. I found death and dying a fascinating subject and talked about it to anyone who would listen. I will say, it can either be a conversation starter or killer at a cocktail party. When talking about the topic of people dying, one must curate their audience carefully. Some people are very interested to hear about it; others, not so much.

I've been with literally thousands of dying people as a hospice nurse, and I can confidently say that most dying people get to a place of acceptance by the time they die (though this is not always true of their loved ones). Many dying people are very ready to be out of here. I can recall only one time where acceptance only came in the final moments of life.

Warren was a young man, in his early forties, with lung cancer. I'm unsure why he had no visitors, but he was alone in our care center that afternoon. He was really struggling, first to breathe, which was relieved when I gave him some morphine, then with fear, which I assumed at the age of forty-two was about the thought of no longer existing. This is the quintessential definition of existential suffering, which is not something we can medically manage. I could throw morphine at this guy all day long, but that wouldn't alleviate his distress over dying. All I could offer was my presence.

Rosie, the hospice aide, had joined me in the room, and we were positioned on opposite sides of the bed, each holding one of his hands. I could see on Rosie's face the same look that I knew was betraying me and exposing my powerlessness. No matter, though—Warren was not focused on either of us. Instead, he had what we call the death stare. The vacant, glassy-eyed look I had first seen in my patient with the nun visitors and many times since. It is a look that is the perfect representation of the adage "The lights are on, but nobody's home."

For several minutes that seemed like an eternity, Warren just kept struggling, like he was trying to live or trying to die. Suddenly, his eyes darted up toward the ceiling, their glassy appearance shifted to laser-like focus, and I have never found any way to describe what happened next other than a look of peace washing over his face. And then he died. The experience was more profound than I can adequately or eloquently describe.

I looked over at Rosie. "Have you ever seen anything like that?" I asked her.

The look on her face told me the answer, but she spoke the words anyway. "No, I never have. Have you?" I hadn't, and I've never seen anything like it since.

My death anxiety didn't manifest until I was in my thirties. Truth be told, from the onset of my teen years until well into my twenties, I didn't fear death at all. I welcomed the thought of it. Between the bullying, drug and alcohol issues, mental health issues, and my propensity for finding men who abused me and inability to leave them, I attempted to "unalive" myself several times. ("Unalive" is social media–ese for the word "suicide," because using that can get your video banned.) Nevertheless, I'm fairly certain my mom's reticence to discuss death further than the "sleeping forever" explanation is what ultimately caused me to suffer from an overwhelming fear of dying. I decided to take a different approach with my kids.

In the early-morning hours of my dad's death, I made a phone call to Randy. Laura had joined Mom, Brad, and me at the hospital, and we were waiting for Laura's daughter to arrive. I was so convinced being exposed to death could cure or prevent death anxiety, I made the decision to have Randy wake Eden and Mia, who were fifteen and thirteen, respectively, and bring them to the hospital to see their grandpa one last time. They weren't unfamiliar with the hospital setting; they had both visited him there several times. Eden had even serenaded Grandpa with her guitar. But obviously, this would be a little different, as it was their first exposure to death. Well, the death of a human.

A few years prior to my dad's death, both girls had been

with Mia's cat, Minnie, when she succumbed to liver failure after making a habit of eating plastic (note: keep plastic bags out of reach of your cats!). At the time, I was working at the hospice care center. Eden called me frantically to describe what was happening with Minnie. "She's gasping like a fish out of water!" she cried.

I took a breath and spoke plainly. "Eden, Minnie is *dying.*" I paused to give Eden time to process. After a moment of silence, save for some quiet sobs from Eden, I told her just to pet Minnie and tell her she loves her, and I would be home as soon as I could.

Even though the experience of Minnie's death was traumatic, I hoped that it would somehow prepare them for their grandpa's death, even if just a little. By the time I had called Randy and asked him to bring the girls, Dad had died. When they arrived to the hospital, they didn't seem to find seeing their grandpa's dead body frightening at all. Eden even kissed his forehead. As adults looking back on the experience, both of my daughters have fond memories about being able to see him one last time. As a matter of fact, Eden feels sad for Keith, who lived out of state at the time, for not being able to be a part of the family circle surrounding the deathbed of their beloved grandpa.

Anecdotally, many of my followers who talk about their fear of death have told me it started in their late twenties and thirties. My personal theory is, this is the age when adults truly start thinking about death. When we're kids, we're always waiting for something: waiting for our birthday, waiting for Christmas, waiting to start school, waiting for summer break, waiting to graduate, to turn sixteen so we can drive, to turn eighteen so we're adults, to turn twenty-one so we can drink alcohol. Life moves slowly because we are anxiously awaiting something exciting. Then, as we approach thirty, we recognize we are getting older, and realization sets in about our mortality. I could be right, or I could be totally full of shit. But further evidence to support this notion is Eden, now almost thirty years old, who has admitted to starting to have some feelings of worry about death, despite her exposure to her grandpa's death and having volunteered at the hospice care center as a teenager. However, she does feel those experiences were helpful in minimizing her anxiety.

What I know for sure is fear of death and dying is much more common than I ever realized. It was through my social media that I learned many other people suffer from death anxiety. As I began posting more and more death-related content, I noticed people commenting on my videos that I was helping them to get over their fears.

It was also through my social media and my followers' comments that I realized you don't have to work in hospice to get over death anxiety. For them, learning about the dying process from my education or even just watching my silly videos with dark humor was helpful. At this point, I'd taken a step away from the bedside to work as a hospice quality assurance nurse, which meant my duties were administrative and I no longer did direct patient care. Due to this shift, my own death anxiety had begun to creep back. By no longer being at the bedside of hospice patients, I felt I had lost my connection to death. As strange as it sounds, it was that feeling of being connected to death, thinking about it and talking about it with families, that eased my mind of the anxiousness that had once paralyzed me whenever the subject of dying possessed my mind. I figured that maybe by sharing my experiences, I could help not only myself but others to understand this most misunderstood yet unavoidable journey that every human will embark on.

The conclusion I have reached about getting over the fear of death is that there's only one way: You have to find acceptance that it is going to happen, whether you are actively dying or just worrying about it. It is crucial for those who are in the process of dying, because acknowledgment allows space for better quality of life at the end of life, conversations with the living, closure, and goodbyes. For those with death anxiety, acceptance of death's inevitability seems to suck the power out of it. You don't have to like it, but if you can accept it, you can put it in the back of your mind and move on to other, nicer thoughts. I do recommend you stay away from thinking about flowers. Just in case.

CHAPTER 13

NOT WITHOUT MY DAUGHTERS

Regret can be a major influencer on how a death goes for everyone involved. There can be regret that someone is unable to be with their dying person, such as with Deborah and her dying son, whose wife initially denied her visitation. There might be regret over fractured or lost relationships or about missed opportunities in life. Existential suffering resulting from regret can cause terminal agitation, an end-of-life symptom that can happen to anyone but especially young people with unfinished business. And regret can happen not only over things they wish had happened differently but for a future lost.

I first met Dawn in her parents' living room. At the age of forty-eight, she had successfully staved off her stage 4 cancer for four years by participating in two drug trials. But once the treatment stopped working, her cancer returned with a vengeance, and the family had decided it made the best sense for her to be with her parents, who could provide extra care. The family included Dawn's parents, Joyce and Larry; her daughters, Ashley and Brynna, both in their early twenties; and her sister, Maureen.

Dawn was sitting upright in a floral-print slipper chair, ankles crossed, hands in her lap. Other than being a little pale and slightly thin, she did not look like my typical bald cancer patient. Once the chemotherapy had stopped working, her hair had grown back quickly, and she wore it in a cute pixie style. She had wire-framed, Coke-bottle-lens glasses that magnified her blue eyes, giving her a somewhat childlike appearance. She spoke slowly and articulately as she reached across her chest toward her left shoulder with fingers splayed. "I really need this taken out."

"This" was an implanted chest port, an intravenous device used for infusing medications. She felt it was paining her, and she wanted it gone. The topic of the port would become the theme of our visits for several weeks until finally I relented and called her oncologist to arrange to have the port removed. I had hesitated because I felt it was more likely bone metastasis than the port that was the source of her discomfort. I was concerned that as her cancer progressed and caused her more pain, we would need that access to provide her with the medications she would require. Unfortunately, I wasn't wrong.

Over the next few weeks, Dawn's condition worsened, and I began visiting more frequently. As is often the case in hospice, when the patient begins to decline and sleep more through the visits, the hospice team's relationship with the family begins to develop. Dawn's family wasn't hard to get to know. Joyce and Larry were in their sixties and obviously devoted to the youngest of their two daughters. Larry was a tall man with a slender build. I would learn later that he had been a raging alcoholic for years until Joyce gave him an ultimatum—he would quit, or she would leave. She was serious and he knew it. He never touched a drop of alcohol again after that day twenty years before.

Having had a history with alcoholism myself, this little fact triggered a thought I often had: *How much sobriety would I have if I had never started drinking again?* I did a mental calculation—*fifteen years, yep, that sounds about right.*

Maureen was close to my age. I became her confidant as she shared her sadness with me in a way she felt she couldn't with her family members. This dynamic was a little unusual, as it is typically the social worker who provides the emotional counseling. However, it isn't out of scope for a nurse to provide support, and the social worker, Lizzy, had her hands full with Ashley and Brynna. Actually, it's not a fair assessment to say her hands were full, as that would imply that they were challenging, and they were anything but. These girls had been living with the potential death of their mom looming large since they were teens and had developed remarkable coping skills for their young age.

Patients with cancer will often experience increased pain as they approach the end of their life, and Dawn was no exception. Despite having her port removed, Dawn suffered greatly from continued pain in the area where it had been. Not only were high doses of oral pain medications not helping anymore, but Dawn was also having more difficulty swallowing them, another common end-of-life issue. I realized we were going to have to find an alternate route of medication delivery, and since we no longer had the port, a subcutaneous infusion was our only other option. The subcutaneous infusion, or Sub-Q as we call it in the biz, is delivered by a tiny little needle that goes just under the skin. The needle is removed, leaving a catheter much like an IV, and we can deliver highly concentrated opiates or other meds. Because it is so little, the procedure to put it in is quite painless. So, after obtaining an order, I popped a Sub-Q site into Dawn's left thigh and started an infusion of the narcotic Dilaudid, a big gun, something sure to ease her pain.

At first, it seemed the infusion was keeping her pain under control, but after a few days, even with steady increases in the drug rate, Dawn, who now had begun to get a little incoherent, was starting to get restless. The one drawback to Sub-Q infusions is, because the space is small, we are limited in how much we can infuse before the body stops absorbing it. We had now reached that point with the Dilaudid, and so it was decided a second infusion was going to be necessary. So, in went another Sub-Q site, this one in her right thigh.

As the days went by, Lizzy and I spent more time in the kitchen with the family while Dawn slept. Joyce would often put out fancy plates of nuts, cheeses, and fruits that we snacked on while we chatted about everything from how well Dawn's pain was managed to what we would do should that no longer be the case. I definitely got the sense this family would be willing to do anything to ensure Dawn would never have to experience pain or suffering again. Our visits became longer as Lizzy and I provided more emotional support to Dawn's family and increased management for her worsening symptoms.

Before we had started the pain pumps, Dawn had been taking methadone, which is used in hospice to treat pain. But because she was having difficulty swallowing and we figured the Dilaudid would control her pain, we stopped it. Now, the two pumps were maxed out on the dose that could be delivered, and she was starting to show signs of pain again. I consulted with our pharmacist, Christy, who decided we would need to restart the methadone. The problem was that Dawn wouldn't be able to take it orally. Hospice treatments are often on the cutting edge; we sometimes step into uncharted territories with medication administration and uses. Methadone infusions were something that had been done on occasion, and Christy had researched the literature enough to feel confident this would be an appropriate next step for Dawn's treatment. So, I placed a new Sub-Q site into her upper arm, and a methadone infusion was started.

One day, Ashley bounced into the kitchen and tossed a small parcel onto the counter. "Mom got another package," she announced with a giggle.

I glanced up from my laptop to see Larry pick the package

up, shake it, and then squeeze it gently. "Hmm, I wonder what she got this time," he said, smiling. Even though Dawn's family had made me feel like I was one of them after the weeks we had spent together, this was an inside joke, and I didn't know the punch line. The perplexed look on my face must have conveyed my curiosity, so Brynna filled me in on the details. Dawn had developed a habit of online shopping late at night after her pain meds had kicked in. Due to the nature of having been a little altered at the time of her purchase, she would often forget what she had ordered. Sometimes she even forgot she had ordered anything at all. It had become a source of comedic relief for Dawn to try to guess what was inside her mystery packages before opening them. But now, Dawn couldn't open her package or share in the laughter. She was sleeping most of the time. When awake, she was restless and incoherent, speaking only garbled nonsensical words or not talking at all. Larry ripped open the padded envelope and pulled out the contents: an infinity scarf. These endless knitted circular scarves were all the rage. He chuckled half-heartedly. "She always wanted to be fashionable."

As the days wore on, Dawn's periods of restlessness became more frequent, more prolonged, and more severe. She moved about in the bed constantly and tried getting up often. She was far too unsteady and weak to be allowed to try to walk, though. So after a couple of exhausting days for the family, who were taking turns sitting with her, I decided to see if we could give her the Haldol tablets from my comfort kit of emergency medications, crushed and mixed with a little applesauce. As I mentioned before, Haldol can be very effective to treat agitation. It would have worked for Dawn, too, except she had now completely lost her ability to swallow, and the disgusting mixture of drugs and fruit stayed pocketed in her cheeks until we scooped it out with a sponge on a stick. At least the three pain infusions seemed to be doing their job. Although she was agitated, she was no longer crying out, writhing in pain, and holding her shoulder. So, after ruling out any other source of discomfort, I felt certain Dawn was experiencing terminal agitation.

I stood at the kitchen counter with Dawn's family. The same counter we had stood around day after day to talk about how to manage Dawn's symptoms, enjoy the gourmet treats, or just shoot the breeze. The same counter where, just days ago, we had laughed about Dawn's new infinity scarf and her habit of online shopping under the influence. Today the mood was much more somber, and a heavy sadness permeated the air. In the past, when we had talked about what to do should Dawn's symptoms become unmanageable, the family, especially Larry, had adamantly insisted she would stay at home. I hesitantly broached the subject of transferring her to a higher level of care in an inpatient setting. Hospice care facilities, often called hospice houses, are not available everywhere; however, they lived in a metropolitan area and there was one available. No matter, though—Dawn's family had not changed their position. This was the family home, and this was where she would die.

Maureen had been sitting with Dawn, who was finally sleeping peacefully for a moment. Overhearing the conversation, she joined us in the kitchen. "We can't just let her suffer. So what are we going to do?" she pleaded. This was my cue to bring up a rarely utilized option in the home: palliative sedation. This type of sedation was reserved for the most extreme cases of agitation, and I had no doubt this was the direction we were heading in. The family knew Dawn well enough and loved her enough not to want her to remain in such an agitated state any longer. If sedating her was the answer, that was what they agreed we should do.

I made the necessary calls to get the ball rolling for the infusion. I consulted with our hospice pharmacist and medical director and afterward obtained orders from Dawn's oncologist for the infusion. Midazolam, otherwise known as Versed, would be our drug of choice. This benzodiazepine, often used for conscious sedation in medical procedures such as colonoscopies, was excellent for palliative sedation. It worked fast, was able to be delivered subcutaneously, and had a short life. This meant that if the family changed their mind, we could stop the infusion and the patient would wake quickly. Of course, that's assuming they weren't in the dying process, in which case they would remain unresponsive.

Before submitting the prescription request to get the medications delivered, it was my responsibility to obtain informed consent. I gathered the family in the kitchen and explained to them the principle of the double effect; although it was our intention only to sedate Dawn until her natural death, the procedure could result in hastening her death. If that were the case, we would never really know because, as I told them, Dawn was already beginning the dying process. There were no questions, and Larry, whom Dawn had designated her power of attorney, took the pen and set the tip on the paper. Before he could sign the first letter of his name, we heard Dawn's high-pitched voice wailing from the back bedroom.

"I don't want to leave my daughters!" We all stood frozen for what seemed like several minutes until Brynna rushed down the hall to comfort her. Ashley quickly followed suit, with Maureen just a few steps behind. I searched Larry's face for any sign of doubt about the sedation. He stared at the entrance to the hall contemplatively.

Moments later, Maureen reappeared. "We have to do this," she said, brushing tears from her cheeks. "She will fight until the end if we let her, and she doesn't have anything left to fight with." She was right. Dawn had become a shell of her former self, and the fact that Maureen was advocating for sedation was impactful, as she had been the most conservative about medications throughout Dawn's hospice care. Larry, never having removed the pen from the form, signed his name.

I didn't waste any time contacting the pharmacy to have the medication, pump, and supplies delivered. Two hours later, I was popping in a fourth Sub-Q site and pushing the sequence of buttons on the pump to get it started. With a whirring noise, the medication began to slowly infuse into Dawn's tiny body. It would be a while before it took effect. At eight that night, I left the house in Seattle and climbed into my car. It was nine thirty by the time I finally made it home to Tacoma, after fighting through the perpetual I-5 traffic.

Normally I was very good at emotional boundaries and not taking my work home with me. This night, however, I couldn't help but think about Dawn and her family. I wondered what the night held for them. I had reminded them to call hospice any time during the night if the medication wasn't working, and I hoped they would do it rather than trying to hold down the fort until I returned the next morning.

After a restless night, I woke early and took my coffee to go. I had already arranged with my manager to have my planned visits for the day taken care of by a float nurse so I could do an eight-hour shift of continuous care to manage Dawn's symptoms. When I arrived at the house, everyone was up, sitting in the living room and drinking coffee. Everyone except Brynna. I immediately knew by the tired faces where she was. I walked down the hall to find her standing next to her mom's bed.

"No, Mom, you can't get up," she told her, placing her hand on Dawn's shoulder. "You're too weak, you'll fall." As she carefully started pushing her back down by her shoulders, I stepped forward and grabbed Dawn's feet, swinging her leg back up onto the bed.

"I take it the sedation isn't very sedating?" I asked Brynna.

"Yeah, not so much," she replied as she pulled the covers up over Dawn. "We ended up calling hospice last night and the nurse had us increase the medication, but she's still"—she turned and motioned to Dawn with her hand—"like this." Dawn had settled into the bed briefly but was already starting to try to get up again. I picked up the pump that was infusing the Versed and checked all the settings. Everything there was fine. The dose, which had started at two milligrams an hour, was now at four milligrams, just as the night-shift nurse had instructed. I traced the line back to Dawn's arm, where the Sub-Q button was still intact—no problem there either. It had been approximately four hours since the dose had been increased, so I knew I could go up on it again now. While Brynna held Dawn's hands, trying to keep her from standing again, I increased the rate to five milligrams an hour.

At first, I was hopeful, as Dawn began to calm down almost immediately. But half an hour later, she was up and down again, like a yo-yo. I could sense the frustration her family was feeling, especially Maureen. Being the big sister, she was starting to exhibit the signs of survivor's guilt, something that often happens when an older person outlives their younger family member.

"Watching her be so uncomfortable is like torture," she said, pacing around the room. "What is next if this doesn't work?"

I walked over to her and placed my hand on her shoulder. "We have more medications we can use," I reassured her. "I'm just going to step outside and make a phone call."

Once again, I called Christy for guidance. This time the order I received was for phenobarbital subcutaneously. This is a drug I used frequently when I worked in the hospice inpatient setting in my earlier nursing years. I knew if this didn't work, nothing would. Because phenobarbital can be damaging to tissue, it has to be given in the form of an injection every eight hours. I would get Dawn started on it and then arrange for another nurse to relieve me at the end of the day and stay overnight.

Like the Versed, the phenobarbital calmed Dawn immediately. But this time, it seemed to last much better. At five that evening, my relief nurse arrived—Karen, an LPN. I handed off all the information she would need to care for Dawn during the night. Four infusions: Dilaudid in each leg, methadone in her right upper arm, Versed in her left upper arm, and phenobarbital injections into her belly every eight hours. I headed home.

The next morning, I walked up to the house to find the front door open. It was a beautiful day. The air felt calm and peaceful as the sun cast small squares from the screen door into the entryway. I was pleasantly surprised to find it was just as calm inside as it was outside. As usual, everyone was having coffee in the living room, but they actually looked refreshed. Karen had kept Dawn sleeping all night by administering the phenobarbital, and while she slept, so did her family.

Dawn appeared very peaceful. Her face was relaxed, and she was so still. I picked up one of the pumps and started recording and clearing the settings while Karen gave me her report. As she dumped urine from the bag of the catheter I had placed several days before into a container, she told me, "Nothing to report. I mean, she was a little restless just after you left, but I gave her the phenobarbital, and that last dose did the trick."

I looked up from the pump to see Maureen standing in the doorway. She was watching Karen pour out the final drops of urine from the catheter bag. "Do we have to keep the diaper on?" she asked. Even though Dawn had a catheter in, the hospice aide had placed an adult brief on her the day before in case she had a bowel movement. "I feel like it is so undignified," she said. I told her we didn't have to put one on her; we would just put her in panties and if she soiled, we would clean it up. "Thank you so much," she said, looking relieved.

Speaking of cleaning her up, now that Dawn was so comfortable, I decided it was time to do just that. Several days of agitation had prevented us from bathing her, and she was starting to smell, well, if I'm keeping it real, a little ripe. I summoned Brynna and Ashley to the bedroom. "Would you like to help me bathe your mom?" I asked them.

"Can we do that?" Ashley replied. "I mean, we're not going to hurt her by moving her, are we?" She looked worried. I assured her the medications were finally keeping their mom comfortable.

I filled the pink basin with warm water and rinse-free body wash, then proceeded to direct Dawn's daughters on how to bathe her. I moved the multiple infusion lines out of the way while the two girls sponged warm water over her body. Washcloths moved in circular motions down her arms, across her chest, where the scar of her port removal remained, and over her belly, marked by tiny scattered bruises from phenobarbital injections. Dawn lay motionless, breathing easily, further testament to her comfort. Ashley and Brynna reminisced about their life with Mom. "Remember when we were little, and Mom would put us in the bath together?" Ashley said.

Her comment invoked a memory of bathing my own two daughters together. Eden had adamantly refused to continue the practice at the age of four, after Mia filled the tub with brightly colored puke from the *Blue's Clues* birthday cake she had overindulged in. I won't get into specific gory details, but it wasn't the first time Mia had subjected Eden to bodily excretions in the tub.

Brynna nodded. "Yes, and now we are bathing her," she said. Once Dawn's body had been cleaned, I assisted them in washing her hair. After we finished, Ashley grabbed a comb and styled it. "There, just like Mom likes to wear it!" Now that she was clean, the girls wanted to put lotion on her. Ashley selected a bottle from the variety of fragrances Dawn had on her dresser, and both girls rubbed a deliciously floral lotion on her arms and legs.

Just as they finished, Brynna looked disappointed. "We should have put that one on her," she said, pointing to a bottle that had "angel" in the name.

"It's okay," I told them. "The one you chose smells amazing."

It was time to dress her, and the girls giggled with delight as they picked out her favorite pink T-shirt and leopard-print panties. Getting a T-shirt on a motionless person is always difficult, and even though Dawn was tiny, she was no exception. I grabbed my bandage scissors out of my bag and carefully split the shirt up the back to the neckline—a trick of the trade. Then I was able to easily slip it over her head and pull each arm through the sleeves. "There," I said with satisfaction. "She looks beautiful." Both girls stared at their mom silently, faces beaming. Finally, Brynna spoke.

"Something is missing," she said. "I know!" She snapped her fingers and turned around, bouncing out of the room. When she returned moments later, she held a wad of fabric in her hands. Ashley and I began laughing at the same time—it was the infinity scarf. Brynna lovingly placed the scarf around Dawn's neck. "There," she said, "now she's perfect." It was time for me to leave, and I wondered if I would see Dawn alive again. Tomorrow was Saturday, and although I would be working, I felt certain Dawn would not live much longer.

The following day I woke up early and flipped open my laptop. As I perused through the emailed death notifications, I spotted Dawn's name. I felt relief but also a little disappointment as I realized my time with her family had come to an end. I always say it's not sad when a patient dies, because this is the expected outcome. If you've made them comfortable and educated the family on what to expect, it's a job well done. Toward the end of a person's life, they become unresponsive, and as a hospice nurse, I'm not really interacting with them anymore at that point. However, I do continue to have a relationship with the family, so it's them I miss. Dawn had only died a couple of hours ago, and the family, knowing I was working that day, requested I do the time-of-death visit. They were okay with waiting for me to get there.

I hopped in my car and drove over to Dawn's parents' house one last time. I was surprised to see cars lining both sides of the street so early in the morning. After finding a place to park, I walked up to the house. Once again the door was open, and I could see many people milling around inside. Apparently, once the family had notified their closest friends, many of them had arrived at the house to congregate in what became an informal wake. I walked down to Dawn's room, where her body lay in perfect stillness on the bed. I didn't need to put my stethoscope on her chest to know she had died. Her eyes were partially open, her jaw was agape, and her skin had a waxy appearance. I had seen enough dead bodies to know that look. I opened my laptop to chart my final notes. Then I closed the lid, placed my computer back in my bag, and made my way down the hallway to say my goodbyes.

If we are lucky, we might get to experience something during our lifetime that is so sacred it feels divine. For me, being able to provide Dawn's two young daughters with the opportunity to perform her ceremonial last bath was one of those times.

CHAPTER 14

THE NEED TO KNOW

In 2010, my dad was diagnosed with idiopathic pulmonary fibrosis (IPF), which loosely translated means, "We don't know exactly what caused your lung disease, but you definitely have it." We all knew, though. It was from his lifelong habit of smoking cigarettes and exposure to whatever things jet mechanics are exposed to.

IPF is a serious, often terminal respiratory disease, and a few months after his diagnosis, Dad ended up in the hospital. At first, the doctors thought it was pneumonia and told us a round of antibiotics should "clear it right up." But it didn't. He just kept getting worse, and I, along with my mother, stayed at his side. Any time I could grab one of the hospitalists, I would try to pin them down on what was really going on. "I'm a hospice nurse," I would tell them. "I can take it." Still, they were very optimistic, even when he ended up with a bacterial lung infection that had a 50 percent survival rate. He did improve for a few days, and I took the opportunity to make the two-hour trip back home to relieve Randy, who had been handling the parenting duties of my teenage daughters.

My time at home was short, though. Just two days later, my dad had a major respiratory crisis and ended up in the ICU on a BiPAP, a kind of breathing support machine you wear over your mouth and nose. I jumped in my car and headed back to the hospital. I'm pretty sure I cut the drive time in half.

My mom was standing next to the bed when I arrived, my dad sitting up. "They said I might have a year left, and they're talking about hospice," he said, his voice muffled by the oxygen mask.

I was confused. "That doesn't make sense. Hospice is for six months or less," I told them both.

"We think you need to call Dad's regular doctor," Mom said.

A few minutes later I was on the phone with his pulmonologist. "Is it time for a hospice consult?" I asked, and finally received the affirmative answer I had been expecting weeks ago.

Medical advancements have taken death out of the home and tucked it away in hospitals. We've created euphemisms like "passed away," "gone to heaven," or even "celestial discharge"—yes, that's one I've heard. Ask any hospice nurse what they think about the phrase "they've expired," and they will tell you people aren't milk.

"Death" is not a dirty word. It's a normal part of life, and yet it's been turned into a taboo topic.

People seem to think that saying words like "death," "dying," "died," or "dead" will cause it to happen. Death is what it is, and calling it by another name won't change that outcome. But even doctors avoid the D-word. If you're not a healthcare provider and you want to tell people your person is "with the Lord," I don't have an issue with that. It's your person, you're free to choose your words (although, I'm just going to say it again: it doesn't make them less dead).

It's imperative, however, when healthcare professionals are dealing with people experiencing the emotional distress of their person dying, that they leave no uncertainty about the situation. It is absolutely possible to be honest and use appropriate and concise language to deliver bad news compassionately.

When those seemingly gentler ways of describing death are employed, though, it can cause confusion. Fear of the term increases fear of the thing itself.

Truthfully, a dying person's prognosis is often the elephant in the room. Although nobody wants to talk about it, everybody wants to know. If they don't ask, it's because they're usually afraid of the answer. Families don't want to bring it up to the dying person because there's a common fear it will take away their person's hope, making them die faster. I'm here to call bullshit on that. On the other hand, the dying person sometimes doesn't want to bring it up to their family and bum them out, which, of course, it will. My advice? You're dying, so they're going to be bummed either way. At least getting the subject on the table will allow for meaningful conversations that might not happen otherwise.

I do many TikTok livestreams wherein I answer questions people put in the comments. During one of these sessions, a young woman asked me how she could get her husband to acknowledge that she was dying, because she really needed to talk about it. I advised her to be straightforward with him and tell him what she needs. After all, she was the one dying, not him. Thirty minutes later, she hopped back into the comment section and said she had left the live to go talk to him, and he'd agreed to stop shutting her down.

It's not always the family or the dying person who doesn't want to talk about death, though. Many times, doctors themselves don't feel comfortable broaching the subject. After one frustrating encounter, a nurse colleague walked back to the team station shaking her head. "You are not going to believe what Dr. Halpern just did," she told me. "She told the family in room twelve that their mom had *gone to heaven*."

I knew from the chaplain assessment and through chats I'd had with this family that they were not religious, least of all were they Christian. And they were all grown adults, not that it would have been more appropriate to say if they were children. "What did they say?" I asked, incredulous.

"They just looked at her dumbfounded. And then she said it again!" she told me. "Then one of them asked her what she meant, and she finally said, 'she died.'"

More often, this comes up before the patient has passed. I've had lots of patients and family members ask me that magic question, "How long?" Obviously, death is unpredictable, so it's not always possible for even the most experienced healthcare provider to offer a definitive answer. However, using our experience, clinical judgment, and observations of the normal end-of-life changes in the human body, we can give an estimate of how much longer we think a person will live. Sometimes we're right and sometimes we're not even close. I'd like to say when we're right it is because of our expertise, though sometimes I think it's just a crapshoot.

Right or wrong, the important thing is to avoid avoidance. It's through open and honest dialogue that a more peaceful, and even *beautiful*, end-of-life experience for all involved parties can begin. Conversations with dying people go so much better when thoughtful, informed discussion can take place— as opposed to leaving us nurses flying by the seat of our pants because the doctor forgot to mention the most significant thing about hospice: that all roads lead to death.

To be fair, up until recently, medical school didn't include education and training on how to talk to people about the fact that they're dying—and I still don't think they spend much time on it. Our healthcare system is driven toward curing illness and preventative medicine. People who become doctors usually do it because they want to save lives, so that's what their education and training is focused on. That being said, all doctors who refer patients to hospice should understand that it is not curative care or preventative care. It's end-of-life care, and that is what they need to tell patients *before* sending them to us.

I stood at the nurses' station, matching the bubble-packaged medications to the orders the doctor had written, before placing them into the brown paper grocery bag on the counter in front of me. I was only about halfway through the meds, a pile of medication cards still lying on the counter, when Raven walked up for our daily chat. She held a coffee cup in her hand and was wearing a fluffy pink robe that highlighted the youthfulness of her rosy cheeks. At twenty-eight years old, with colon cancer, she was the youngest patient I had cared for so far.

"Good morning!" she greeted me joyfully. She was obviously in a happy mood due to the fact that she was going back home today.

"Hi, Raven! I was just packaging up your medications that you'll take with you," I told her as I placed another card in the bag.

Raven scanned the counter, looking at the remaining stack of medication cards and then back to the paper bag. Her face suddenly changed from delight to distress. "Those are all for me?" Now she looked like she was about to cry. "I was hardly taking *any* medications before I came here."

Raven had been admitted to the care center just about a week ago to have her bowels managed. She had become so severely constipated, due to a partial bowel obstruction and the opioid medications she was taking for pain, that she'd required medical intervention to clean her out. After successfully treating her with a variety of medications, enemas, and finally manual fecal disimpaction, she was to be released home along with the pile of medications she was observing me bag up, which would prevent her from having more of the same issues in the future.

"Raven," I said slowly, trying to convey as much compassion as I could—which wasn't hard, because I truly felt compassionate toward this young woman. "It's so important for you to be on a bowel protocol so you don't end up in here again." Raven stared at me quietly, her eyes starting to glisten with tears. I solemnly continued. "The doctor thinks you have weeks to months left."

Raven began to yell as those darn tears suddenly broke free and flowed with full force down those darn rosy cheeks. "Weeks to months," she cried. *"Weeks to months?!* The doctor told me I had a year left!"

Goddamn oncologist, I thought.

Time and time again, patients referred to hospice are told they are going there because "they can give you extra help." The doctors fail to mention to the person that they are dying, let alone that their life expectancy is only six months or less. This happens with enough frequency that we almost always assume all patients admitted to hospice might not know exactly what it means. On one hand, I guess you want a doctor who is treating your life-ending disease to be optimistic for your best chance of survival. But there comes a time when it's imperative to replace optimism with reality. It's an injustice to a dying person to not be truthful about how much time they might have left. One can't work on a bucket list if they don't even know they are expected to kick it in the near future.

I carefully tried to explain to Raven that hospice was for patients with a life expectancy of six months or less. Of course, we couldn't know for sure how long she had, but the doctor wouldn't have referred her here if they didn't think that was the case. Unfortunately, that did nothing to ease her suffering. Eventually, I summoned the medical director, and we held a care conference to get her on the right page.

Dr. Sawyer was a hospice doc extraordinaire, who started her career as a nurse and worked her way up to a doctor. The role of hospice doctor suited her quiet, patient demeanor perfectly. After their meeting ended and Raven returned to her room to finish packing, I apologized to Dr. Sawyer and was met with grace. "It's not your fault, Penny," she told me in her soothing, quiet voice. "This is what happens when we fail to address the reality of the situation. Everyone deserves to know the truth."

Raven was young. I understood that it would be difficult for her doctor to talk to her about her life ending, even though it was *their job*! Again, prognostication can be challenging, especially when the person is further away from death. As they get closer, though, it's more obvious, and that's when I really get pissed that the doctors have failed to give a heads-up to the patient and family. Sometimes the family *does* actually want to know.

On another day, I had been waiting most of my shift for my admission to arrive from the hospital down the street when the back door alarm alerted me that someone needed to be let in. I glanced at the camera and saw two men in EMS uniforms with a gurney.

I headed down the hall and held open the door as they pushed my patient past me. "Room eight," I said to them, "on the left." One of the men picked up an envelope that had been lying on top of the patient and handed it to me. I already knew from reviewing his hospital record that Mr. Thompson, a patient with end-stage lung cancer, had signed a DNR (do not resuscitate) advance directive. That document was pretty much a moot point; Mr. Thompson looked very close to the end of his life. No amount of CPR would do anything to revive him. I pulled the lime-green POLST (Physician Orders for Life-Sustaining Treatment), a type of advance directive used in the state of Washington, out of the envelope. I could see the name "Rebecca Thompson" scrawled on the signature line.

Rebecca, his wife, had driven herself over from the hospital and arrived just as we were sliding her husband onto the raised-up bed. I could tell in one quick glance that she had to have spent days in the hospital at her husband's side. Her hair was disheveled, and the purple top she wore was slightly wrinkled, likely from sleeping in the uncomfortable recliner the hospital provided for visitors. She looked exhausted and worried.

"Are you Rebecca?" I asked her.

Rebecca had been watching intently as the medics slid a blue transfer board under her husband. "Yes," she said, not turning around while her unresponsive husband was placed in the hospital bed. "I'm his wife."

I reached out and put my hand gently on her shoulder. "Has anyone told you how long he has to live?"

She shook her head. "No, and I need to know!" she exclaimed, finally turning around to face me.

I didn't bother with giving her a time frame, it was too close to even call. "Don't leave," I told her. He died within the hour.

One of the greatest gifts life has to offer is the ability to acknowledge that it is ending. That is the only way to ensure meaningful conversations, closure, and goodbyes. As a hospice nurse, I will die on that hill. No pun intended.

CHAPTER 15

JUST A TASTE OR TWO

Something so many people get so wrong about hospice is that they think we make people stop eating and they starve to death. It is true that we teach people never to force or coerce their dying person to eat. Trying to convince a dying person to eat sets up stressors for everyone involved. We educate about this ad nauseum and still witness family members desperately trying to get food into their dying person, often saying, "You need to eat to keep up your strength!" as they attempt to shovel food into them. No, they don't need eat. They're *dying*, and they aren't dying because they're not eating. They're not eating because they're dying!

Of course, some dying people enjoy eating. On a quiet Sunday at the hospice care center, I made rounds checking to see if our patients who were still able to eat wanted something for dinner. Dotty Williams was a somewhat salty lady who made no apologies for her gruff demeanor. She had been a life-long smoker with no regrets despite her diagnosis of a type of lung cancer that left tumors protruding from all parts of her body.

"What would you like to eat this evening?" I asked her, following my question with a rattled off list of the entrees made available by our chef before he had departed for the day.

"You know what I would really love?" she asked. "A grilled cheese sandwich. I love grilled cheese, and it's been forever since I've had one." I assured her I could make that happen and set off to the kitchen.

Being in somewhat of a rush to start on my evening med pass, my grilled cheese skills were somewhat lacking that day, and I ended up with a slightly charred sandwich. Not wanting to make Dotty wait any longer and needing to get back to the nurses' station, I delivered the sandwich with my apologies. "I can make you another one if this is too burned for you," I told her sheepishly. But she was content to go ahead and eat the inferior product I had served her. Later that evening, as I made my final rounds, I asked Dotty how that sandwich was.

"It was the best grilled cheese I've ever had," she told me earnestly, smiling. It was also the last grilled cheese she would ever have. When I returned to work after a few days off, Dotty's room was occupied by a new patient.

Giving food to a person is something anyone can do; you don't have to have any medical knowledge or expertise. For the family member who feels so helpless and wants to do something, anything for their dying person, feeding them seems like the easiest thing to do and the right thing to do. Especially because we associate a good appetite and eating with wellness. After all, who doesn't believe on some level that chicken soup is the ultimate remedy for a cold? So one of the most challenging aspects of being a hospice nurse is getting people to understand that a dying body doesn't *need* food.

Almost all family members want to be able to hold on to the hope that their person will live as long as possible, that somehow they will miraculously get well. And even those families who are resigned to the fact that their person is going to die no matter what still don't want them to die from starvation, which is thought to be painful. But here's the thing: not eating is part of a natural death. It isn't painful. These people aren't like the people on the Greely Expedition to the Canadian Arctic in the late 1800s, who were stranded without food and willing to eat anything for survival—including their boots and their dead party members. These are people who are dying a natural death.

So, in order to understand why a person who's dying doesn't need or often even want food, it's important to recognize what the actual purpose of food is. Obviously, many of us like to eat. We love the taste of food, we like to socialize over a meal with our friends. We use food to celebrate: birthdays with cake, anniversaries with dinner in a fancy restaurant, and weddings with hors d'oeuvres or buffet-style meals. Even wakes after a funeral offer appetizers. For many people, food equals love, which makes it even harder to accept that a person doesn't want to eat.

But the fundamental reason that we need food is that it acts as fuel for our bodies. And what does fuel do? It keeps things running. When a person is dying, their body is shutting down. It isn't trying to run anymore; it isn't expending energy and therefore doesn't require calories or nutrition, aka fuel. So, it sends the message that they don't need to eat.

Another problem with eating is that it involves digestion, which is a huge energy-consuming process. When a body is preparing for death, it goes into energy-conservation mode, which includes slowing down digestion. Lastly, food isn't always appealing when you are sick—something we've all experienced. There are many disease-related reasons that can cause a lack of desire to eat. For example, medications (especially chemo drugs) can change the taste buds, nausea or vomiting can curtail the appetite, and people who are dealing with pain just might not feel very hungry.

All that being said, if a person wants something to eat, like Dotty with her craving for a grilled cheese sammie, we are not going to deny them. Hospice nurses encourage recreational eating and comfort foods, letting patients indulge in whatever their heart desires. If they want to have ice cream for breakfast, that's okay. If they don't want to eat anything at all, that's okay. And if they only want a taste or two, that's okay too.

Prior to the gastric cancer that cost one of my patients his digestive system and a one-hundred-fifty-pound weight loss, he had been obese. Seeing this man who was extremely thin, it was hard to believe he had ever been overweight. But it wasn't a stretch to imagine that he had been a self-proclaimed "foodie" because, in spite of his illness, he still loved to eat. Unfortunately, this was problematic. I don't know exactly what the surgical procedure was, but basically, most of his stomach and part of his intestines were removed, leaving a stoma in his small intestine, which, again, is basically a hole in his abdomen out of which anything he ate would immediately exit, only partially digested, into a bag. If he ate a sandwich, a chewed-up sandwich came out. If he consumed french fries, whole pieces were in the bag. If his last meal was a cheeseburger, out it came, pickles and all. And everything was mixed with fully digested food . . . poop. Because of the volume of food and waste, it was impossible to make a regular ostomy appliance work for him. So instead, he had a drainage system that used a large tube connected to a catheter bag. It would have worked well if he could have stuck to a diet that leaned more toward being pureed or liquid. But he loved food, and who were we to deny a dying man whatever he wanted, even if what he wanted usually consisted of meat and potatoes?

One day, after having enjoyed a meal of a cheeseburger and fries, the tube connected to his drain bag broke apart for the umpteenth time, pouring chewed-up food mixed with liquified shit all over the floor. After the hospice aide and I took care of the mess and were back at the nurses' station, she began to grumble. Now, I love hospice aides. Most of them work very hard and don't complain, including the one I was working with that day. But after a few times cleaning up similar incidents, she had reached her limit.

"Someone needs to tell him he can't eat like that anymore!" she ranted to me. I empathized with her. It was, after all, literally a shitty job.

But I told her, "He is dying, and we are here to make sure his last days are the best he can hope for. So we will continue to give him what he wants, and we will continue to clean it up."

The aide looked down at the floor. "I know," she said apologetically.

***

I learned about the importance of recreational eating several years before I became a hospice nurse, when Rayna was dying. She had always been very concerned about her appearance. As I mentioned before, she was a model in her younger years, and even at age fifty-six she kept her five-foot-nine body svelte through fanatical exercise and a diet that limited her from eating anything that wasn't perfectly healthy. I remember meals at her house always included something she had doctored to have less calories, and eating out with her at restaurants was always a puzzling experience to me because she would only order the lowest calorie food on the menu. To me, there is no point in eating at a restaurant if you aren't going to pig out on good food.

I once met up with Rayna in Seattle on a business trip for dinner at 13 Coins, a restaurant known for its amazing Australian lobster tails. She ordered one but asked them to hold the butter. *Who does that??* I thought. *Who doesn't want to drown their lobster in butter?* She deprived herself during life to stay fit, but that changed when she learned she was dying. A few weeks before her death, she decided she wanted a cheeseburger. A *bacon* cheeseburger. "I haven't allowed myself a cheeseburger in years, and I want one today," she told her husband, who dutifully rushed right out and got one for her.

Now, let me tell you, she loved that cheeseburger. All two bites of it, which was literally all she ate. Her husband was very upset by this. "She asked for a burger, so I drove to the place and bought her one," he told my then-husband and me, angrily. "And then she only ate two bites!"

But his anger wasn't about the trouble and expense of getting her a burger. His anger wasn't really anger at all; it was disappointment, despair, and grief as he was having to come to grips with the reality that his wife, the love of his life, was really going to die. At the end of the day, it didn't matter if she ate two bites of a burger or the whole thing or ten burgers; that food wasn't going to change the path she was on. But damn, she sure did love having those two bites of that bacon cheeseburger, and that was valuable information that I took with me into my practice as a hospice nurse.

So, contrary to the strange belief that hospice nurses starve their patients, I have found that being able to give a dying person whatever they want, especially when it ends up being their last meal, is one of the most satisfying parts of my job. And it was most satisfying during a time when it wasn't a part of my job.

In the ICU, before my dad was officially on hospice, the doctors drastically limited what he could eat and drink. He had developed medication-induced diabetes, so he was on a diabetic diet, which he absolutely hated. My dad was a big man who grew up poor and *loved* to eat, so food restrictions never went over well with him. He had also developed a syndrome that required fluid restriction, and he was miserable. "I'm so thirsty," my dad would complain to my mom as she reminded him that he couldn't have any more than four ounces of the Dr Pepper that sat on his overbed table.

When we finally got his hospice referral, I picked up that

can of Dr Pepper and started pouring it into his cup. "But he's not supposed to have any more right now," my mom told me worriedly.

"Mom," I said, "he's going on hospice now. He can have whatever he wants." Then I picked up the phone to call my sister, Laura, and instructed her to "bring Dad a venti Starbucks, STAT!"

An hour later, Laura and I were at the Golden Corral, a restaurant I refer to as a meat buffet. We piled a to-go container high with roast beef, burgers, fried chicken, and every other meat they had available. Oh, and we got a salad for my mom, who proudly considers herself almost a vegetarian. We returned to the hospital with the food and left my mom and dad to have a nice intimate dinner together. Well, as intimate as one can have in the buzzing, beeping ICU of a hospital. My mom later told us he ate every bit and enjoyed it to the very last bite.

Like Dotty with her grilled cheese, that meat buffet would also be my dad's last meal, because he died that night. In the depths of our grief, grasping for some comedic relief, my sister and I joked that we might have inadvertently pushed him over the edge with that huge meal. But even if we did, we weren't sorry about it. For my dad, suffering was being denied food and drink, and at least we'd sent him on his way with a full belly.

**

Just as digestion slows down during the dying process, so does the circulation of body fluids. Add to this a decreased ability to swallow, which is prevalent in most people as death approaches, and you have someone who is going to get dehydrated. But again, contrary to popular belief, dehydration is not a bad thing when a person is dying. Too much fluid on board can cause extreme suffering, as the inability to circulate those fluids causes them to build up around the heart and lungs. This can lead to shortness of breath and sometimes chest pain. It's for that very reason that we don't turn to IV hydration when a person stops taking oral liquids.

If a person can safely swallow and indicates they are thirsty, like with food, we will never withhold something from them. As their swallowing begins to fail, though, they are at risk for aspiration. Aspiration is when the liquid goes down the wrong way and ends up in the airway or the lungs. At best this is uncomfortable; at worst it can cause aspiration pneumonia—which, for people who are ready to check out, isn't necessarily a bad thing. (Ever heard the adage "pneumonia is the old man's best friend"?) Once we explain the risks, if a person is alert enough and can manage a sip of water, ice chips, or a Popsicle, that is perfectly fine.

There is also the option of thickened liquids, but we generally don't do this because . . . gross. Thickened liquids are for hydrating people who are trying to live longer and who are willing and able to get past the disgusting unnatural texture that thickener adds to something that is inherently supposed to be liquid. Again, dying people don't need those liquids as they are nearing the end. However, that isn't to say I haven't happily thickened a beverage when a patient requested it: coffee, cola, and even one time beer, an IPA, if I recall correctly. But they usually report they are less than pleased with the end product.

Sometimes a dry mouth can be mistaken for thirst. If you've ever smoked pot and had cotton mouth, you know that uncomfortable sensation. It doesn't matter how much water you drink—you'll still feel like someone poured sand in your mouth. If a person absolutely can't swallow or aren't very alert, oral care with a sponge on a stick (toothettes, they're called) or a soft toothbrush moistened with water will be their best friend. Like those who got creative with the thickener, some of my patients have used those little sponges to moisten their mouth with non-water substances. Beverages with alcohol in them generally should be avoided, as they are going to be more drying. But if a person is alert enough to ask for a little dab of whiskey on their tongue, do it!

So, yes, there is a risk that a person who is dying, their swallowing function failing, might inhale something into their lungs and develop pneumonia. But sometimes the benefit is worth the risk, such as when you are a dying old man and you want a Popsicle.

One morning I walked into the room of one of my new patients, Marcus, who had come over from the hospital late the night before. His daughter was with him, and I introduced myself and greeted them. "How are you both doing?" I asked.

His daughter got up from the recliner she had been seated in. "I'm okay, but he would love a Popsicle," she said, gesturing toward her dad with an outstretched hand.

"I can get him a Popsicle!" I offered.

"Well, the nurse last night said he can't have one because he might aspirate on it," she told me.

I looked at Marcus and back at his daughter. I shrugged my shoulders to convey the unspoken message that we should give him what he wants. "He's on hospice," I said.

"That's what I thought too!" she exclaimed.

I asked Marcus what kind of Popsicle he wanted, and a few minutes later I handed him blue raspberry, as requested.

Later I went back to check on Marcus. "How did you like that Popsicle?" I asked him.

He looked up at me with the biggest smile on his blue-stained lips. "*So* good."

CHAPTER 16

HANGING ON

People want to avoid death at all costs, and sometimes the price tag is very high and ultimately defeats the purpose. It's incredible what a person will put their body through to try to eke out just a few more days.

Against my experienced advice, my own father took chemo drugs and steroids because they offered an extremely slight chance of prolonging his life. I knew those medications had side effects and could not only poorly impact quality of life but possibly even shorten it. In his case, that was exactly what happened. He developed an infection secondary to his crappy immune system due to the medications that promised to extend his life.

However, regardless of how I (the person not dying) felt about the decisions my dad (the person dying) was making, at the end of the day, it is each person's own life and death. They deserve the autonomy to choose their path, and as hard as it may be to support their decisions when we disagree, it is the right thing to do. Of course, ensuring that they know all the pros and cons is an important consideration to being willing to provide that support.

Something my social media followers are always surprised

about is that a person on hospice can have a full-code status. This means healthcare professionals initiate resuscitative efforts (cardiopulmonary resuscitation, aka CPR) to try to restore life to a person after they have died. "What's the point of that," my followers will ask, "if they're about to die anyway?" Great question, and the answer generally goes back to doctors not wanting to talk about anything involving possible death to their patients. Medical shows depict CPR as a miracle procedure that can restore life without consequences. In reality, CPR can cause fractured ribs, and when done on a hospice patient—if it even works—they are still going to be dying. Only now, they are dying with added pain from the physical trauma of the CPR. A patient can also choose a code status of do not resuscitate (DNR), which is the only instance in which medical providers will not do CPR if a patient stops breathing or their heart stops beating.

Hospice providers are very good at explaining what a full-code status and CPR really mean, and we don't turn people away if they choose to be full code. In fact, Medicare requires that we do not. In my experience, hospice providers do try to keep the conversation open, however, and continue to provide information and answer questions in case a patient wants to change their code-status decision. Usually, they will, but occasionally patients adamantly remain full code.

My home-care patient Gordon was a great example of this. He was in his early fifties, with colon cancer and multiple gastrointestinal fistulas (think holes in the belly that leak out poop constantly—fun). Gordon was African American and had an inherent mistrust of the predominantly white healthcare industry, likely due to the known racial disparities in quality of care. He was a full code and wouldn't even entertain a conversation about it. I had to work very hard to gain Gordon's confidence, but he also had an excellent sense of humor. Every visit

I made for the first three weeks as his case manager started with him asking about my chickens, which he had seen on my laptop screen saver.

"Hi, Gordon. How is your pain today?" I would ask.

"The more important question is, how are those chickens of yours?" he would reply.

Gordon had been a weight-lifting champion and proudly displayed a framed picture of his glory days on his wall. In the photo, he was very handsome, posed in a squatting position, with hands on a heavily weighted barbell resting on the floor. He wore a yellow singlet with a belt that had a massive buckle. The muscles bulging from every part of his body in that picture now belied the frail human he had become.

He was still a very proud and independent man, though, which was both admirable and annoying. He lived alone, and although he had some support from his mom and sister, they were often frustrated with his reluctance to make any plans. Neither were willing or able to commit to full-time caregiving when he started to need extra help. That was completely reasonable, especially since his sister had her own health problems and his mom was in her eighties. Thankfully, after a month of us getting to know each other and my earning his trust through our chicken chats, I was able to persuade him to accept a hospice aide.

Whenever I had a patient who lived alone, I liked to have an aide visit frequently so another set of eyes could be monitoring them. My aide was a gorgeous, petite Ethiopian woman named Lily. Although the primary purpose of a hospice aide's services is to assist patients with hygiene, many people aren't ready to give up their independence with more intimate care. Often I would have a very frank discussion with the patient, pointing out that when they inevitably got to a point where they could no longer care for themselves, it would be less awkward for them if they knew the person who would be giving them a bed bath or wiping their ass. (Although my choice of words was always much more professional unless the relationship I had developed with the patient allowed for such language!)

In Gordon's case, however, he couldn't imagine a time when he would need any help. Even though he took no offense to foul language and used it often himself, my frank approach was not working. Instead, to get Lily's foot in the door, I promised him she could help with household chores. So, twice a week, Lily would go to his house and do such things as take his garbage cans to the curb, wash dishes, or put in a load of laundry. I knew if anyone could get him to accept help with his hygiene, it would be Lily. I had already experienced her work magic with other stubborn patients by doing simple tasks and bonding until they were open to more intimate assistance.

Gordon had been on service for about three months when I pulled my Prius into his driveway, a nursing student with me. I knocked on the door and heard a feeble, "Come in."

I pulled the screen open to find the door was locked. "Gordon," I yelled, "the door is still locked."

I could hear his muttered annoyances and shuffling footsteps as he approached the door. After what seemed like several minutes, the door flung open, and a skeletal man waved us in. "Come in, ladies," he said, turning away from the door. To say he was skeletal doesn't begin to describe how emaciated his body had become—which was saying something, as he'd already been skinny when I met him. We followed him into the living room, where he sat on the couch and turned his attention to my student.

"Is this the new one you're breaking in?"

I plopped down on the couch next to him. "Yep. Jody, meet Gordon." He nodded at Jody in acknowledgment, but when he didn't bother to offer his hand, Jody reached hers out to him.

Gordon ignored the gesture and turned his attention to me. "How are those chickens of yours doing?"

I motioned to Jody to sit in a chair across the room. "Still cranking out more eggs than I know what to do with."

Gordon leaned back, smiling. "I keep telling you to bring them to me. I know what to do with them!"

I opened my laptop and started typing in my password. "Now, Gordon, you know the rules," I playfully chided him. "If I give them to you, I have to give them to all my patients. Then I won't have any left for myself!"

Gordon snorted. "Oh, right. I forgot about the hospice code of egg giving," he said sarcastically and in good humor.

Once I was ready to take notes, I started asking Gordon questions. "How's your pain today?"

He replied, "It's been better," and when I asked for a number, he began to grow visibly irritated. "I don't know . . . You nurses and those numbers. Can't I just tell you it hurts a lot?" I understood his frustration. Even though I was taught this method to do a pain assessment, it never made sense to me. I might say I'm a ten with the same pain that another person would rate at a five. It's too subjective, in my opinion.

"I agree the numbers are kind of stupid, but I'm supposed to ask," I told him. "More importantly, though, how much oxy have you been taking?" I continued. He had been prescribed oxycodone tablets for breakthrough pain, to be used in addition to his long-acting morphine.

Gordon reached for a notebook. "It's all written down here, just like you asked me to do." I was surprised he had actually done something I suggested.

While I took the list from Gordon and started adding numbers up, he turned his attention back to Jody. "What do you do?" he asked her.

"I don't . . . What? Sorry, I'm not sure I know what you mean." Jody looked puzzled and startled by the sudden attention from our gruff patient.

"For fun," he clarified. "Like where do you hang out?" He looked her up and down. "You into fitness at all?"

I looked up from the notepad at Jody and motioned with my head to the picture on the wall. "Gordon used to be a bodybuilder," I told her.

She got up and walked over to the wall where the picture hung. "Wow, that's a great picture," she told Gordon.

"Yeah, what you really mean is, 'What happened to you?'" Gordon replied, not unkindly but in a matter-of-fact tone. Jody looked mortified. Gordon smirked at her. "It's okay, I'm just messing with you. That's an old picture. People change, right?"

I set down the notebook and picked up my laptop again. "Okay, Gordon, you know the drill. Tell me what's been going on."

Gordon answered the routine questions. "Appetite fine, sleeping fine, no falls. It's all good. I'm fine."

I typed in my laptop. "Bowels?"

Silence.

"Gordon, bowels?" I repeated.

"Fine," he said.

"Wounds?" I continued.

"Also fine," he answered.

"Mind if we take a look?" I asked, setting my laptop down on the coffee table. Gordon sighed and glanced at Jody, then hesitantly reached down and lifted his shirt up, revealing several brown-stained bandages on his abdomen.

"You just had to show me off to the new girl." He nodded toward Jody. I could sense his embarrassment.

"I'm sorry, Gordon. This is purely professional," I reminded him. I had called ahead of the visit to get his permission to bring someone along, but I should have realized his pride might get a little bruised. Despite his deteriorating appearance, he still considered himself to be a ladies' man. He had even attempted to hit on me once, but I quickly redirected him by flashing my wedding ring and nurse's badge at him.

I told him I should probably change the dressings. "Yeah, let's just get it over with, the stuff's on the nightstand, you know where." I returned with the wound-care supplies a few minutes later, and I could see Gordon and Jody were both relieved I was back. As much as Gordon liked to act tough, he was fairly shy until he got to know a person. I was sure as soon as I'd left, the room had just overflowed with awkward silence.

I set the supplies on the coffee table: a spray bottle of wound cleanser, several packages of thick gauze, bandage scissors, and a roll of paper tape. I reached into my pocket and grabbed a small bottle of hand sanitizer, first squeezing some on Jody's already outstretched hands, then on mine before rubbing them together. Once they were sufficiently dry, I reached into my bag for some clean gloves.

"You want to do the honors?" I asked Jody, handing her a pair of gloves and gesturing toward Gordon. She smiled, trying to look confident while pulling on blue medical gloves. She proceeded to slowly remove the bandages, revealing rotten-looking tumors oozing a foul-smelling brown liquid. She took a quick short breath, held it, and turned her head away from Gordon. She did her best to hide the repulsed look on her face but was betrayed by a little retching noise that escaped.

"It's the stuff that dreams are made of," Gordon quipped.

We finished up our visit and left Gordon sitting on the couch. "See you next week, Nurse Penny, and don't forget to bring me those eggs!" he called out through the screen door as we climbed into my car.

"So, he was . . ." Jody started.

"A little offensive?" I jumped in. "And I know you know I'm not talking about those wounds."

Jody leaned back in her seat. "Well, I was going to say 'interesting,' but since you said it first, yes, he was kind of rude."

I nodded in agreement.

"But you didn't seem to be too bothered by it," she continued.

"Yeah, well, the guy is my age," I explained, "and he's going to die of a horrible cancer that's robbed him of his looks and his physique, which I think you could probably tell he prided himself on. I guess I feel like even though he can be a real butt, he gets a pass."

Jody was silent for a moment. "Those wounds were so awful," she said, shaking her head in disbelief.

"Yep," I acknowledged. "It's amazing how the body can destroy itself. They don't really teach you about that in nursing school, do they?"

The next time I saw Gordon was only two weeks later, but he had changed drastically. If he was skeletal before, I didn't know what I'd call him at this point. His eyes were bulging out, his lips were drawn back over his teeth. Basically, he looked like the walking dead. The wounds had grown, and he complained he was having to change the bandages constantly. We had tried attaching colostomy bags to his abdomen to contain the liquidy stool, but they just wouldn't stick. Worse than that, his pain had become so severe that even the very high doses of opioids he was taking weren't able to keep him comfortable. It didn't help that he still lived alone and was having more difficulty remembering to take his meds. It was time to come up with an end plan.

When a person is on home hospice and simply needs more help, an inpatient care center is the best way to go. I knew of a beautiful facility, where I had referred patients before. In fact, it was where Rayna had gone to die. It wasn't easy to persuade Gordon he needed more care, but his pain outweighed his apprehension, and he agreed to go. He would go to the care center, but he still refused to change his code status from full code to DNR—or to even discuss it. That would be a bridge I would have to cross later. For now, I knew it was imperative to act quickly to get him to the facility before he changed his mind and was less willing to leave his home.

Once he had been in the care center for a few days, his pain had become well managed on a morphine infusion. Typically, when a patient is in a care center on a higher level of hospice care, the goal is to return them to their home once their symptoms are under control. Having no caregiver doesn't factor into that decision at all; this level of care is for symptom management and only meant to be short term. In Gordon's case, however, the massive tumors protruding from his body that required frequent dressing changes continued to qualify him to stay. Thankfully, he had not attempted to initiate any conversation about going back home.

I had known Gordon for only a couple of months, but it felt like it had been a lifetime. He was one of my all-time most challenging patients. He could be arrogant and narcissistic. He was also one of my favorites, and at one visit, I knew it would be the last time I ever saw him. It was the Thursday before Memorial Day weekend, and I was going on a four-day vacation. I paused at the doorway and watched him for a moment. I could see he was still alive by his protruding ribs rising and falling with each breath. *What is he waiting for?* I thought. There was absolutely no way he was going to live much longer.

His face was turned toward me, and suddenly his eyes blinked open. "You just gonna stand there all day?" he asked weakly. I walked into the room and sat down next to him. "Did you bring me some eggs?" he said, smiling gently.

I chuckled and shook my head. "No," I said quietly.

We sat in silence for several moments, and then he spoke. "So I guess you're going to be gone for a few days, right?"

I nodded. We had already talked about my upcoming trip to a beautiful cabin in the woods with my husband just a few days ago. We both knew this was goodbye. I told him what I've told many of my patients at this point in my relationship with them, "If I don't see you again, good journey to you."

He thanked me for everything I had done for him and asked me to thank Lily too. I was a little surprised by his offer of gratitude—he'd never thanked me before. I shook his hand and left the room.

I tried to leave the building but found I just couldn't. I had a nagging thought I couldn't quite let go of: *Gordon is still a full code.* Despite having attempted to discuss his code status on numerous occasions, I was never able to sway him from his decision. I marched back into his room.

"Gordon," I said firmly, "I just can't leave here knowing you are a full code without discussing it one more time." I proceeded to lay it all out on the line for him. "When your heart stops, they will pull your body out of this bed onto the floor and start CPR," I said seriously. "Look at your chest—you are fragile! They will break your ribs and rupture all of those tumors." I held nothing back and was met with silence but only for a moment.

"Penny. Tell me something," he said. "Is this a good place to die?"

I pointed out the window to the birds on the bird feeder, the trickling fountain, and the manicured gardens beyond. "This is the *best* place to die," I told him.

He smiled impishly, almost as if his decision to hold off so long had been calculated just to torment me. "Okay," he said. "Bring me that piece of paper, and I'll change it."

Four days later I sat on the porch at our cabin while Randy loaded the last of our luggage into the car. The weather on the mountain had been perfect, and I had welcomed the reprieve from work. But I couldn't stop myself from checking my work email each day to see the death list. Every time I logged in, I had scanned the list over and over to be sure I hadn't missed Gordon's name. I hadn't. He was somehow still alive, and for some reason, I just couldn't bring myself to see him again. "Guess what?" I said to Randy. "I'm going to call in sick tomorrow, so let's stay another day."

The next morning the weather was just as beautiful as every other day had been, and as I looked up at the blue sky, I saw a golden eagle flying overhead. There are lots of birds up on our mountain—eagles, ravens, hawks—so it wasn't unusual to see one, but the peace I felt it bring me told me Gordon's journey had come to an end. Sure enough, his name was finally on the death list.

I later learned from the social worker that Gordon's estranged son had made a visit to the care center to see him. I was shocked; he had never mentioned having any children to me! When his son got there, Gordon was barely responsive. His son spoke to him, forgiving him for not having been more of a presence in his life. In my hospice career, there have only been a few times I've seen or heard about dying people doing what Gordon did next. He told his son, "I can leave now," and then he died.

People like my dad, who intentionally try to hold on to life through medical intervention, are one thing. When it comes to the natural dying process, that is a different story. I heard a hospice doctor repeat this saying once: There are two sides to dying, the physical side and the spiritual side, and both must meet before death can occur. I'm not sure who the original author of that phrase is, but I've found it to ring true many times. I've seen people who were physically ready to die but hanging on, like Gordon, and those who couldn't wait to get out of here but whose bodies weren't quite there yet. Once Gordon had the peace he needed through forgiveness from his son, he was finally able to let go.

***

Similarly, when my dad realized his attempt at living longer was futile, he too had a quick departure. In the years since I had begun working in hospice, I had become an RN, and later I would even go on to get my bachelor of science in nursing, or BSN. But just that morning, the plan had been for me to take my dad home the next day so I could be his personal hospice nurse.

After spending all day at the hospital and ensuring my dad got his feast, my siblings, Mom, and I headed for home—Laura to her house, and Brad, Mom, and I to my parents' house. Mom looked depleted as she dragged herself up the stairs of their split-level home. "I'm going to bed," she told us. Brad and I headed the opposite way, down the stairs to the family room. Brad, ever the night owl, plopped down in front of the computer to peruse the internet, while I crawled into Dad's hospital bed, which was still parked in front of the big-screen television.

I was still trying to process all that had happened that day. It was a normal day in terms of how many hours were in it, twenty-four, just like every other day. Yet somehow it seemed to both drag on and fly by at the same time. It was just that morning that, *finally*, I'd reached Brad on his cell phone. He had celebrated his birthday a few days before with a trip to Canada and hadn't been answering. *Finally*, after weeks of reminding the doctors what I did for a living, they decided hospice was the right next step, and we'd gotten the consult. Dad *finally* got his huge cup of joe, and *finally* each of us took turns for our last conversations with the beloved patriarch of our family. Mine went like this:

Dad: You did it, Penny, you really did it. You became a registered nurse, and I'm so proud of you.

Me: Thanks, Dad. That means a lot.

Dad: I guess I must have been an okay dad, because you all seem to love me a lot.

Me: You're the best dad, Dad.

Dad: I want you to have the car.

Me: The Enclave?!

Dad: No! Do you know how much that car cost? You can have Mom's Oldsmobile.

Me: You can't blame me for trying.

Have I mentioned humor is a great coping mechanism?

Back at my parents' home, I pulled a fluffy down comforter around my neck and gazed up at the ceiling. A beam that spanned the ceiling had been spiked with pegs, where hats upon hats hung above me. *Look at all the hats,* I thought, admiring Dad's baseball caps, cowboy hats, golf hats, and a Stetson. *There are so many hats hanging up there.* My dad was a collector of many things and apparently, I'd just realized, he was obsessed with hats. *Look at all those hats hanging up there,* I thought again as I marveled at the impressive display of his chapeaus. The phone rang, interrupting my hat pondering.

It was the nurse calling. "I think you should come to the hospital," she told me.

I didn't ask any questions. "Okay," I said and hung up the phone. I told my brother we needed to go and ran upstairs to get Mom. She had been so exhausted by the day she hadn't even changed into pajamas, so she was ready to go. We hustled down to the car and climbed in, Brad driving, me in the front passenger seat, and Mom in the back behind me. We were about halfway to the hospital when Brad's phone rang. With one hand on the steering wheel, he fumbled around, pulled his phone out of his pocket, and tossed it to me.

"Hello?" I answered.

"Is Brad there?" I immediately recognized the woman's voice on the other end—it was the nurse.

I told her this was his sister, whom she had just spoken to minutes before. "What's going on?" I asked.

A moment of silence before my family's world changed. "Your dad just died."

So much for the plan.

When we arrived, his nurse asked me if I wanted to know how it happened. I wondered if she asked everyone this or just me because she knew I was a hospice nurse. In my own nursing practice, I've found that people often want to process the death of their person. I almost always call families after their loved one dies to ask, "How did it go?" This allows them an opportunity to work through the details of the experience with someone they know won't be intimidated by the forbidden topic. Now, being on the receiving end of that conversation, I was no different. "Yes," I said.

The nurse said he had started having some trouble breathing, so she went to get him some morphine. When she got back to his room, he told her, "I'm about ready to hang it up." She gave him the morphine and went back for some Ativan. He died moments after she returned to him.

I instantly realized it was likely at the very moment that my dad was telling the nurse he was about ready to hang it up that I was lying in his home hospital bed, gazing up at his ceiling, thinking about all his hats hanging up there. Coincidence? I know what I think, but I'll let you determine your own conclusion.

As I've said, saying your last words and immediately dying happens rarely in hospice. That's more of a Hollywood thing. Most of the time, people who die a natural death go through a progression of symptoms in a dying process that can be quick or lingering. A dying person can linger for a number of reasons, and as much as this can upset the family, which is often waiting for things to just be over, lingering doesn't necessarily equal suffering.

I always say death takes as long as it takes. It can take too long, or it can happen too fast. Either way, it never happens at a good time. Even if you go out like my dad, saying, "Check, please!" and exiting shortly thereafter, let's face it—dying is inconvenient.

CHAPTER 17

THE WOO-WOO STUFF

"Is there an afterlife?"

Many people on social media ask me that, as if by virtue of being a hospice nurse I'm some kind of an authority on what lies beyond. Others assume that someone living a life devoid of religion can't hold a belief that there's something beyond our life on Earth. It's true that having no formal religious upbringing, I had no concept of an afterlife. But working with the dying presented me with an opportunity that would change my beliefs: deathbed visions.

Lena, Mrs. Jones's daughter, called me into room seven. "I think Mom needs some medication or something. She's hallucinating," she said worriedly. Mrs. Jones was lying in her hospital bed, staring up toward the ceiling, pointing at the air, and uttering something quietly. I couldn't quite make out what she was saying at first, but as I continued to watch and listen, I heard a name: Winnie.

I turned to Lena. "Who is Winnie?" I asked.

Lena looked at me, puzzled, and then as if a light bulb had turned on, she said excitedly, "Her sister . . . my aunt . . . Aunt Winnie!" Her excitement turned back to confusion. Frowning, she told me Aunt Winnie had died last year.

Our conversation was interrupted by Mrs. Jones, who

continued to point and was now clearly calling out names, "Momma! Hi, Daddy." I explained to Lena we did not need to medicate her mom. These were deathbed visions.

"Deathbed visions" is a misleading misnomer because they can happen weeks before a person's death, before they are even on their deathbed. Sometimes, this phenomenon is also called end-of-life visioning. It is very common that a dying person will say they see their deceased loved ones or even pets. I once spent a fair amount of time helping a patient look for the cat she said she was seeing in her room before she admitted that she realized it had been a childhood pet. Sometimes it happens in dreams, sometimes it's right in front of them, as for Mrs. Jones. Witnessing this mysterious end-of-life phenomenon, or even just hearing about it, can be life-changing. These visions bring comfort to the patient who experiences them, to the family who sees their dying person "reunited" with their lost loves, and for the death-anxiety sufferers like me.

One evening, I was hammering away at my computer keyboard, documenting notes, when I suddenly heard a voice cry out.

"Ingrid! Ingrid!"

It was coming from the room next door to the nurses' station, where I sat. My patient John was in his eighties. His wife had died from cancer the year before he landed in the hospice care center with an end-stage terminal heart condition. John had been married to her for decades. They had no other family except for their private-hire caregiver, Josie, who had lived with them for several years before his wife took ill and with whom they had become very close.

"Ingrid! Ingrid!" I heard again as I stood up and hastily went to see what John was so upset about. John was lying in the hospital bed, reaching up toward the left corner of the room. Tears were streaming, no, pouring down his cheeks. "Ingrid! Ingrid!" he cried out again.

I walked up next to his bed. "John?" I said gently. "Was Ingrid your wife?"

He stared intently at the corner. "Yes!" he yelled, almost startling me. "*Yes*! And she's right there. I can see her!" By this point in my experience with dying people and deathbed visions, I believed those they said they saw were there. Curious to know if Ingrid had any insight into how soon John would die, I asked him if she was coming to get him. "*Yes!*" he said again. Then he smiled and calmly added, "But not today. Tomorrow."

Wow, I thought. *That was very specific.*

The next day was Monday, and—drum roll, please—Ingrid did *not* come to take her beloved husband to wherever it is we all end up. Instead, he died two days after he had seen her.

A week later, Josie came to pick up his belongings. I excitedly told her about John's visitor and how Ingrid had said she would be coming to get him Monday, but then he didn't die until Tuesday. Without missing a beat, Josie said, "It was always like Ingrid to be late."

That certainly left me with plenty to think about.

As I said, visioning brings comfort to dying people and their families—usually. Occasionally, though, people can be a little thrown off by it. Like Mrs. Jones's daughter, they often think their loved one is experiencing hallucinations that require medication. Some medications or disease processes can cause people to hallucinate at the end of life; however, that is different than visioning. Hallucinations almost always cause distress, and we will intervene by assessing the cause and providing medication to relieve any anxiety or fear the person may be suffering from. But if the patient isn't afraid, once we point out to the family that these visions are normal and bring peace to their person, they are usually okay or even enthralled by the occurrence. I also steer loved ones away from redirecting their person by telling them no one is in the room. Let them see what they see. Who are we to tell them that their beloved person really isn't with them?

Sometimes, even patients can be caught off guard by their visions. They don't always recognize the people, or they could be just shadows at first. They might even be reticent to talk about them because they aren't sure how people will receive that information.

My patient Florence was in her eighties and dying of a lung disease called chronic obstructive pulmonary disease (COPD). My visits took place in her home, where we always sat at her kitchen table. From time to time during my patients' stay on hospice, I like to check in with them about things that can help guide me to where I think they are in their dying process.

"Have you had any falls?" I asked.

"No."

"How much are you sleeping?"

"A lot."

"Eating?"

"A little."

"Have you seen any unusual things you want to tell me about?"

Florence paused. "Seeing things like what?" she asked.

"Oh, like deceased relatives or pets?" I replied.

"Oh no!" she said hurriedly. "Nothing like that."

I explained to her that it wouldn't be unusual to see something out of the ordinary. "It's normal for people who are dying to have visions like that," I calmly told her.

"It is?" She sounded incredulous. "Well," she said slowly, "my dad is standing over there in the kitchen." I knew without looking that there would be no one there, but I turned around to see an empty kitchen anyway. "I was afraid to say anything because I thought you might think I'm nuts!" Florence exclaimed.

"Nope," I told her. "It's perfectly normal." And I knew that meant the end was near. She died about three weeks later.

Whether they believe in them or not, people are fascinated by stories of end-of-life visioning. Those who do believe don't question that the dying person really is seeing their deceased loved ones. Those who don't believe love to toss out theories to rationalize and explain them away. Social media commenters will insist it's just hallucinations from the medications, their disease, or DMT. I can easily dispute they are caused by medications or disease. I have seen many patients have visions who had no brain involvement in their disease. Some have never had so much as a drop of morphine or any other medication that is known for hallucinatory side effects.

When it comes to DMT, however, that one is a little more interesting to me. DMT, or dimethyltryptamine, is an organic hallucinogen that occurs naturally in many plants and animals, humans included. I used to just dismiss comments about DMT out of hand, vehemently denying it as a possibility of the source of visions. But, I have to admit, my knowledge was limited to an understanding of the only study ever done, and that was on rats. Apparently, when a rat's death was studied in a laboratory setting, their brains would release a small amount of DMT during the dying process. Obviously, we don't subject dying people to that kind of testing just to satiate our curiosity, so there's no way to know if this same thing occurs in humans. But the people in my comment section surmised that, if it did, the DMT could be the cause of deathbed visions. I was intrigued, so I did a little more googling.

I learned that DMT from plants has long been used by Indigenous peoples as a way to connect with their higher self, their animal guide, or even the spirits of their deceased ancestors, depending on their beliefs. For me, this meant the idea that deathbed visions were either the product of DMT

or actual spirits of deceased loved ones were not mutually ex-
clusive. Maybe DMT doesn't create a hallucination of spirits;
maybe it connects us with them. But in truth, the only evidence I needed was watching people experiencing end-of-life
visioning. Time and again, I've seen patients so convinced
they're being visited by the spirits of their dead relatives, and
that convinces me they really are.

When I met Daniel and his wife, Tina, in their living room,
he proudly showed me an array of Chinese herbal preparations
his relatives had sent him from his homeland. "I went on hospice because my doctor said I should," he told me as he picked
up a packet of herbs and waved them at me, "but I'm not sure
what you can do for me. I'm still going to try to beat this."

"This" was advanced metastatic pancreatic cancer. We
never discourage any home remedies that people want to take
to try to save their own lives. Personally, I've never seen any of
them work, but I'm a hospice nurse, so my patients' survival
rate from cancer is nil.

"Okay by me," I replied. "In the meantime, I will keep coming to see you in case there's anything I can help you with." My
visits with Daniel were cordial, but I did get the sense he had
more faith in his herbal concoctions than in allopathic medicine. Couldn't say I blamed him. After all, he was dying, and
no Western medicines were able to do anything for him. But
as his disease progressed, he started to develop ascites, and the
herbs weren't helping.

Ascites is a buildup of fluid in the abdomen that causes the
stomach to get huge. It's painful and causes difficulty breathing. When people are still able to get to the hospital, we can
have them tapped, meaning a tube gets temporarily put in
the belly to drain off the fluid. While this does relieve the discomfort of the ascites, as the fluid starts to build up more frequently and the person gets more exhausted by the trips back
and forth from hospital to home, it's not optimal to make them

keep going in to have it drained. So, we can have a permanent tube placed into the abdomen that allows us to drain the fluid off in the comfort of their own home. Daniel was hesitant to have the procedure done, but his comfort level was waning, so he agreed. I got the orders from his doctor, and a few days later, Daniel had a drain placed.

As reluctant as Daniel had been, he realized after the first time I drained his belly that this had been a great decision. And I was elevated in status—he called me the best nurse he'd ever had. The drain was easy enough to use that almost anyone could be taught how to manage it. Sometimes family members feel very confident performing the drainage procedure, and sometimes they don't. Tina was a "don't," and that was okay because Daniel's condition was rapidly deteriorating and I felt like I needed to be making daily visits anyway.

It was on a Friday that I knew Daniel was probably not going to be much longer for this world. We had ordered a hospital bed for him, which was set up in the living room so he would be able to visit with his adult children when they came over. He was sleeping when I arrived and barely woke up as I removed the dressing from his abdomen to reveal the tube poking out of his side. I hooked up the vacuum bottle, which quickly started draining the translucent straw-colored fluid. "You doing okay, Daniel?" I asked him.

"Mmm," he grunted.

"Is that a good 'mmm' or a bad 'mmm'?" It sounded like a good "mmm," but I wanted to be sure.

"I'm okay," he slurred. Tina had told me he'd been in pain earlier and that she'd given him some of the morphine from his comfort kit. It was obviously working. I finished the procedure and handed the two-liter bottle to Tina to dump in the toilet. We had been through this enough times that I didn't need to tell her what to do.

I sat down on the couch next to Daniel's bed and opened

my laptop to chart. Tina returned after a few minutes and plopped down next to me.

"I have to tell you what happened last night," she said in a quiet but excited voice. "Daniel told me he could see his mom over there," she said, pointing at the bookcase on the wall in front of his bed. "I thought he was talking about a picture of his mom, but there isn't one there. I told him, 'Daniel, there's no picture of your mom here.'" She shook her head incredulously. "He told me, 'No, not a picture. My mom is standing there, right in front of me.'"

The next day, Daniel died.

Tina called me on the following Monday and asked that I come to see her, as she wanted to tell me how it happened. She said that Daniel told her she needed to call "my nurse." She reminded him I was off that day, but he was very insistent and said he needed me because he was going to die. Tina doubted he was really dying, as he was so alert. She told him again that I wasn't working and she couldn't reach me.

"Okay," he told her. "Then call my kids and tell them to get here." They had two children, a son and a daughter. Daniel's prediction was spot on, and shortly after his kids arrived, he died.

Deathbed visions aren't the only unexplained occurrence that happens at the end of life. Approximately four out of ten dying people will have an end-of-life rally. This is when they appear to be very close to the end of life, then suddenly wake up with a burst of energy. They want to visit, get out of bed, sometimes even eat a meal. As one might expect, when this happens, the family thinks their person is getting better, but in reality, it is a sign that death is very near. The rally usually only lasts about a day or less before they return to their previous state. Then they die within a week or so.

People also often make motions with their hands that may look like they're fishing, smoking, sewing, or other such activities. Although the person can't communicate, family members will usually excitedly state what they are doing. "My uncle was an avid fly fisherman; he's tying flies!" Or "Mom loved doing cross-stitch." One of the most common things we see people do with their hands is reach into the air. I've come to believe this has something to do with seeing those deathbed visions, as they are often above the person or in the upper corner of the room, like where Ingrid was when she was visiting with John.

I'm not trying to convince anyone that there is anything mystical or supernatural, or even that there is an afterlife—we are all entitled to our own beliefs. The truth is, we can only know what happens after we've died, or we won't know anything because there is nothing. And, although that is the very idea my second husband conveyed to me, which, I joke, is what ended our marriage, I can now admit he had a point. I do know, however, that there are people who appreciate these woo-woo stories, and I love telling them. The experiences were cathartic to me. But ultimately, it was my very own spiritual encounter that finally brought me to my personal belief about what lies beyond.

I don't know if my dad had dead relatives visit him, because he died so fast. But *I* had a visit from *my dad* after his death. About a week after he died, my family and I went to my sister's house to camp out for a night. My husband and I slept in one of the guest rooms. As I lay sleeping, I dreamt of my dad. Although I can only describe it as dreaming, it was much, much more. My dad came to me surrounded by bright light, smiling his famous smile, and I could feel his love embracing me. And he was so happy, he radiated joy. He told me it was time to go.

"Okay," I told him. "I'm ready to go!" Then I thought for a second and told him I would need to see my kids again before I went. "They're going to miss me," I said.

"No, it's not your time to go yet," he replied. Then he told me he would always be with me, and he wrapped his arms around me. "I love you, it's all right, honey. I love you, it's all right." I was crying tears of happiness and sadness at the same time.

As I awoke, still sobbing, my husband had his arms around me. "I love you, it's all right, honey. I love you, it's all right, honey," he comforted me.

Strange, I thought. *Neither my dad nor my husband have ever called me honey before.*

"You were talking to your dad," Randy said to me.

"No," I insisted. "My dad was talking to me! I was answering him."

I will never be convinced that what happened that night was only a vivid dream. It was my reality, and I'm so grateful to have experienced it. So is there an afterlife? As far as I'm concerned, yes. Because my dad told me there is.

CHAPTER 18

GRIEF AND THE DYNAMIC OF FAMILY DYNAMICS

"Dan," I said firmly as I placed my hands on the shoulders of my patient's son. "Your mom is *dying*, and if you want to be with her, you *have* to stop getting in the way of her care!"

Although my experience as a bartender was vastly different from being a hospice nurse, I felt the encounters I had when working in bars helped me to feel less intimidated as I faced the towering giant of a man clad in black leather who stood before me. Or maybe it was just that I could see through the gruff façade to a little boy who was desperately grieving the inevitable death of his mom—a reality that was quickly approaching. But let's back up a few weeks.

My patient, Mrs. Dahl, was in her eighties. She had previously lived in her own home, with Dan, her youngest child, as her caregiver. Dan had never married, had no family of his own, and was currently unemployed. I got the sense from his mom that there had been quite a bit of coddling that had stunted his adulting ability. Mrs. Dahl also had a daughter, but she worked in a very high position in a bank and wasn't able to provide much care or even oversight of care.

When I met Mrs. Dahl after she first came onto hospice, she was already bedbound, having suffered a broken hip from a fall. The history I had gathered from the admit nurse was that Dan had been a little unrealistic about the fact that her capabilities were declining due to her advancing dementia. His encouragement for her to "exercise" by walking down and up the steep basement stairs had been the cause of her accident.

Each time I went to see Mrs. Dahl, I found her in a worse condition. Her skin was starting to break down and she was developing open wounds on her buttocks. Although these wounds, caused by pressure from a person lying in one position for too long, can indicate neglect of a patient, this isn't necessarily the case for a person on hospice. The skin is an organ, and like all other organs during the dying process, it will begin to fail. Pressure ulcers can develop quickly even with the best care possible.

For me, the most troubling thing about the care Dan was providing was his reticence to give her any pain medication. He, like many, many family members of hospice patients, was worried that he would cause her to die faster by giving her morphine. I'll reiterate for the people in the back that this couldn't be further from the truth. We medicate people with opioids safely and judiciously, especially if they haven't had a lot of narcotics before. The dose of morphine that had been prescribed for Mrs. Dahl was very low, equivalent to a Vicodin and less strong than a Percocet.

I arrived to find her forehead creased deeply, a sign of pain we look for in people who can't communicate. "Where is the morphine?" I asked Dan. He played dumb, saying he couldn't remember where he put it, until I pressed him into getting the little bottle for me. I tried my best to educate him on the safety of morphine and how much pain his mom was in. "Dan, look at her face—listen to her moaning," I said emphatically as I squeezed a small amount of liquid morphine from a syringe into her mouth. "She's in so much pain."

The social worker, Carlie, and I finally decided we needed

to let Mrs. Dahl's daughter know about our concerns. Although her work had kept her too busy to have much involvement in her mom's care, she really stepped up and took charge once she realized the direness of the situation. Within a week she had obtained custodial guardianship of her mom and transferred her to a nursing home, where she could get better care.

We thought having Mrs. Dahl safely ensconced in a facility would improve her pain management, but unfortunately, Dan was ever present and prohibiting the nurses from giving her pain medications. Even though he was no longer her legal spokesperson, his menacing demeanor made the nurses feel threatened, so they abided by his demands. Once again, his sister sprang into action and informed the staff Dan was no longer allowed to visit their mother. The facility security guard would ensure he did not have access.

By the time Mrs. Dahl had arrived at the nursing home, she was already transitioning. Now, several days later, she was actively dying. With Dan no longer stopping the nurses from being able to medicate her adequately, she finally appeared to be comfortable. But she did seem to be in a holding pattern and unable to let go and die. I made my daily visit to her one afternoon and found her still unresponsive, still looking like she was standing at death's door, but still hanging on.

I was finishing up my assessment of her and heard a commotion coming from the nurses' station just a short way down the hall. Dan had returned and was demanding to see his mom. This time he had a friend with him. It seemed like an effort to show force, but the nursing staff were undaunted and unwavering.

"I'm sorry, sir," an older nurse told him. "We've been told we can't let you in." She turned to a younger nurse. "Please call Rob, the security guard, and ask him to come up here."

"Hey, man," Dan's friend said, "let's just go." He turned to the nurse at the front desk. "It's okay, we don't want any trouble. We'll leave. He just wants to see his dying mother," he told her.

The nurse wasn't moved. "Well, he can't come in because he won't let us take care of her."

Dan looked like he had been physically wounded, but he didn't argue. He lowered his head and quietly left the building.

I followed him outside and found him leaning against a wall near the entrance. This is when I put my hands on his shoulders and emphasized the bottom line. "Your mom is *dying*, and if you want to be with her, you *have* to stop getting in the way of her care! Dan, do you hear what I'm saying?" I asked. My hands were still on his shoulders, and as I looked into his eyes, I could see tears beginning to form.

"I just need to be with her. I need to be able to tell her good-bye." He started to sob quietly, and I could feel my heart breaking for him. "If you can promise—*promise*—that you will not interfere with the nurses medicating or doing anything to care for her," I said, "I can see if I can get you back in to be with her."

Dan's head snapped up. "Yes!" he almost shouted as he brushed off a tear with the back of his hand. "I promise."

After a phone call with Mrs. Dahl's daughter and reassuring the staff at the nursing home he wouldn't be a problem anymore, I guided Dan to his mother's bedside. He pulled up a chair next to the bed and sat down, taking her hand in his.

"I'm here, Mom," he said, gently leaning over and resting his head on her chest. "I love you so much."

I put my hand on his shoulder. "I'm going to say goodbye to you both now." Somehow, I knew that Mrs. Dahl was getting what she needed and that I wouldn't be back.

Dan lifted his head, and for the first time, I could see some kind of peaceful resolution in his eyes. "Thank you," he said quietly.

Thank you, I thought, *for letting my patient end her journey peacefully*. Mrs. Dahl died an hour later, with Dan still holding her hand.

I'm sure it's not going to come as a surprise that working in hospice exposes one to a lot of grief and challenging responses to grief. It doesn't take much imagination to recognize that the death of a person and the grief involved can create a monster of emotional responses from family members. Dan's reactions to his mother dying weren't unique, albeit a little more extreme than most. But there is no correct way to grieve. Grief is as unique as the person who is grieving. Tears, no tears—doesn't matter. How a person responds to their grief doesn't make it more or less valid.

One of the most challenging aspects of caring for dying people is walking into situations where there is a crappy family dynamic or dysfunctional relationship and thinking we can change things. We want to make the dying person's life as good as it can be, and sometimes we lose sight of the fact that there is a whole history of this person's life that existed before we came into the picture.

There can also be confusion, like when someone remembers Aunt Vi looking perfectly healthy three months ago at the family reunion. More than once, I've had someone on the other end of the phone yelling, "What do you mean she's dying now?!" Or there can be harsh judgment or criticism when a family member doesn't want to forgive their estranged or abusive person just because they're dying. (Here's a PSA for you: dying doesn't absolve a person of their sins, and it's okay for people not to want to visit.) As a hospice nurse, when dealing with difficult situations, I've always strived to remember that I am only privy to a very small window of time in my patients' and their families' lives. It's not fair or ethical to judge situations when I don't know the full history.

***

Despite having been with hundreds of grieving families by the time my dad was dying, I wasn't even remotely prepared for what it would be like to grieve the loss of someone so close to me. The impact of his death was like nothing I had ever experienced or imagined at any time in my life. My dad died early in the morning on February 12. When we left the hospital after his death, we all went back to my mom and dad's house—though I guess, officially, it was then just my mom's house. Later in the day, the medical equipment company came to pick up the oxygen and hospital bed. My brother went down to the family room with them, where the equipment was. Moments later, he came up the stairs, holding a pink paper in his hand. He looked stricken. "I was signing the receipt and when I wrote the date down," he wailed, "I realized this is still the day Dad died." This was a sobering moment for all of us. The grief of our loss had been so heavy it felt like it had been dragging for days. But in reality, he had only been dead a few hours.

My siblings and I clung to each other and my mom in an effort to deal with the raw anguish that we all felt. Mattresses were thrown on the living room floor and we camped out for days, processing, grieving, laughing, and crying. Our mutual coping mechanisms alternated between unhealthy (eating junk and drinking cocktails) and healthy (poring over photo albums and videos, choosing the right music for the memorial video we were creating, and planning my dad's celebration of life).

One thing I didn't expect through the grieving process was the physical effect it can have. Once again, I will overshare in the name of educating and keeping it real: I suddenly found myself pooping and peeing constantly. As a lifelong sufferer of chronic constipation, I found this to be very unusual. I kept it to myself, but then when my sister mentioned after a few days that she knew she wasn't ready to go home yet because she didn't even like going to the bathroom alone, we began to compare notes. We learned that we both had been experiencing this increased elimination. A little Google search revealed that stress hormones can be excreted through waste. They forgot to mention *that* in nursing school!

None of us could bear to be alone. We all piled up in the living room to sleep at night—if we even could fall asleep. There was a pattern to our grieving. We would cry together and reminisce on fond memories, we would laugh and crack jokes, bringing levity to the room, and then there would be a long and deep silence. And then someone would cry. And then we would all cry.

On one late night when we all were listlessly making small talk, I heard Eden say, "Hey, guys, do you see that? What is that?" I looked up in the dark from my place in the living room pile of communal bedding to see a lumpy shadow on the chandelier in the dining room.

Laura replied, "Oh, what is that? Yeah, I see it!" We all stared for several minutes, discussing the shape and pondering what it might be. But no one was willing to get up to examine it more closely and solve the mystery.

"Dammit, Brad!" I shouted as it finally dawned on me. "That's my bra!" We all began roaring with laughter, and Brad was obviously pleased with his little prank. After some time, our laughter divulged into more crying as we continued on the roller coaster of grief together.

I don't know how we could have survived without each other. Our grief was such a shared experience, it made the situation so much more bearable. Even after we finally did go to our respective homes, my sister and I often called each other when the grief overwhelmed us. "I'm not doing very good," one of us would say to the other, and we'd cry together.

One of the most surprising things that happened to me was a couple of months after Dad's death. I was sitting in the living room with my husband and Mia, eating dinner and watching *American Idol*. I don't know what set me off, if it was a contestant singing a sad song or a sentimental commercial, but I was suddenly overcome by grief and burst into tears— with food in my mouth. Randy and Mia were in front of me, instantly asking what was wrong. I couldn't even talk because I was sobbing so hard, and I couldn't swallow my mashed potatoes. I was finally able to swallow and told them I was just missing my dad. And that I couldn't believe I had been crying with food in my mouth!

Grief has many faces: sadness (the obvious one), disbelief, and sometimes anger. It's often displaced, as it was for Rayna's husband, who was so upset when she couldn't finish the burger he had gone out of his way to get her. It wasn't about the burger. It was the proverbial writing on the wall that was too much for him to bear.

Grief is nonlinear; it really is like being on a roller coaster. Often people feel like they are through the worst of it, then suddenly they are losing their shit in the supermarket.

The truth about grief is it never goes away; we will always miss our loved ones when they die. But we can eventually learn to live without them. We do what we need to do to survive. As one person I know said about her grief, "I learned how to eat butter sandwiches every day because that was all I could bring myself to eat."

Twelve years after my dad's death, I no longer have to call my sister saying those words, "I'm not doing good," but occasionally that feeling of disbelief that he's gone and how much I miss him still hit me, and I shed a few tears. But never again with food in my mouth.

CHAPTER 19

INFLUENCING DEATH

Okay, I thought as I plucked my phone from the microwave cart, *one and done.* I had no idea how people on TikTok would respond to a story about a dying patient and the nun who influenced my beliefs about the soul leaving the body before death, and I didn't give it much more thought. After adding the hashtags #hospice, #hospicenurse, and as a final thought, #normalizedeath, I clicked Post, put my phone down, and started cooking dinner.

Later that evening, bored without a TV set in our vacation cabin, I clicked on the little black TikTok icon on my phone to let my newfound form of entertainment lull me into mindless relaxation. As the app opened, I noticed there were thousands of views, a fair number of likes, quite a few new followers, and many comments on my very first DeathTok video. Many, *many* comments.

> **@littlebitoluv: Do you think a person can decide their time to go?**

Sometimes it seems they do! I've had many patients who waited for someone to arrive or someone to leave before they died. It seems most of the time they wait for people to vacate the premises. Many hospice nurses have stories of families holding vigil, then stepping out of the room to go to breakfast, and boom, the person dies five minutes later.

> **@therealmrsjay: My daughter is on hospice and we have been told to watch for certain things but I did not know about this. Thank you for what you do.**

Had I started a grassroots movement in death education?

> **@jezusisking: Hospice nurses are angels handpicked from heaven. God bless you, angel.**

I hate to break it to you, but I have a background that might disappoint you.

> **@User32456789345: Years ago hospice was totally different. Why do you think it's ok to give them a shot to put them to sleep?**

Okay, so not everyone thinks we're angels! Also, it doesn't work like that. Are you maybe confusing people with pets?

> **@doodwherzmybeer: Trippy**

I mean, it is an app for youngsters, so . . .

> **@mom0five: I saw that exact look in my husband's eyes right before he passed. It was the sweetest thing, my hand was on his heart for the very last beat.**

There. Right there. That was when I knew that, with this ridiculous app, I could actually connect with others through their death experiences and share the compassion and humanity moments like these have to offer.

After perusing the comments for a while, I shut my phone down for the night. By the next morning, I had accumulated over ten thousand new followers. All at once, I had feelings of excitement and fear. I knew I would need to tell my husband and my employer about this public arena I had just entered. I remembered twenty years back to that website that got much more notice and fallout than I expected. I could find myself in the same boat again. Still, the excitement outweighed the trepidation. People wanted to hear about death, and I had a passion to talk about it. If you want to make it in the social media world, it's important to find a niche, and apparently I had found mine. My niche was death.

As I've said, I am a passionate advocate for death education, which is the only explanation I have for deciding that using TikTok for teaching was a good idea. Knowing that TikTok is primarily used by younger generations and that there are many different learning styles, I wanted to approach my educational videos in a few different ways. Also, not everyone wants a full-minute video about death—let alone three or ten minutes, which is now available on TikTok. They can't digest that information all at once, especially since it is a dark, heavy subject. So, I try to lighten it up. I dance around and point at words or I make jokes; as you now know, dark humor is my jam. I first noticed the impact of this type of teaching when I posted an eight-second video of myself dancing and lip-synching to a song about water. As the song lyrics asserted something along the lines of it being "just water," words I'd added popped up on the screen:

"If your person isn't taking fluids, that's okay."

"They're not going to die from dehydration."

"They're going to die from their disease."

The video garnered over four hundred thousand views, seventy thousand likes, and hundreds of comments, the most notable from a woman who said that for fifteen years since her loved one had died, she'd felt guilty about not giving them water. She had no idea that dehydration was a normal part of the dying process, and I had relieved her guilt. I relieved her guilt with an eight-second video of my dancing around like a fool. Wow!

For the older generations, like mine, who have started finding their way to social media and maybe aren't as savvy to the TikTok trends, I post straight-talk hospice stories and even answer questions from the comment section. Topics range from food and fluids to grief to end-of-life phenomena to CPR, including what it's actually like in real life, which can be violent and traumatic. In an attempt to normalize what a dying or dead person looks like, which is nothing like TV or movie producers would have you believe, I have even made videos where I pretend to be dead or dying to show what a death looks like. I'm so good at it that some people commented my videos needed a content warning!

But influencing death doesn't just happen on social media. It's really more about the impact that we can have on living and dying by approaching both with fearless, open honesty. Not just accepting that death will happen but embracing it and making the most out of the end of life, be it our loved one's or our own.

Hospice care is meant to improve quality of life and bring comfort to the dying. But what is comfortable can only be determined by the person experiencing it. When you are walking the walk alongside someone you love as they journey to the end, it's hard to know how to be with them when they get to the point where they can't tell you what they want. But people typically die how they lived.

Barbara Karnes says there's no such thing as dying. We're born and then we die. We're alive and then we're dead, and everything in between is living. It's hard to know what will bring your dying person comfort when they can't tell you anymore, but if you let that philosophy guide you, you can't go wrong. Someone who wanted to be touched in life will want to be touched while dying, and conversely, someone who didn't like it so much will want you to keep your hands to yourself. If they like lots of people around, they will likely want them there when they're dying too.

In my observations, it seems to be human nature that when someone doesn't know what a dying person wants, they impose their own ideas of comfort. Making assumptions based on one's own preferences can lead to doing the absolute wrong thing. The wrong atmosphere, the wrong type of touch. Don't even get me started on how annoying it looks like it must be when someone incessantly strokes the hand of a dying person, because I would hate that! (See how that works? I wouldn't like it, so I assume others won't either—but some people might actually like that.) And although maybe I'm presuming again by saying that I personally can't think of anything less comforting than harp music, like Lorraine was playing for Brandon, and can't imagine anyone else liking it either, I don't think I'm being overly presumptuous to assume a young man probably wouldn't want to hear it. So the bottom line is, unless you actually do desire harps or choirs singing at your deathbed, tell people what you want.

From the time I started working in hospice, when my daughters were just teenagers, if a song was playing, I would often say, "Make sure if I'm dying someday you play that song for me!" It was usually met with groans of "Mo-oom!" While I was mostly kidding, it is important to know what will bring comfort to your dying person. Make sure music, friends, chatter, smells, whatever, are all things they would find comfortable.

Mrs. Baker was unresponsive and close to the end of her life, at the care center where I worked. But before all that, she'd made sure to let her only child know what her death plan was. I walked into the room to find her adult daughter placing something in her mouth. "What do you have there?" I asked, genuinely curious.

She held up her hand. "Chocolate!" she said proudly. "I promised her I would make sure she got a piece of chocolate each day until the day she died."

Wow, I thought. *I need to remember to tell my kids to add chocolate to my death plan!*

Consideration of atmosphere is important. I've seen patient rooms crowded with friends and family and loud music playing or football on the television, while my patient lay captive, actively dying. When I ask if that's what they think their person would like, someone will usually embarrassedly turn the volume down and escort people from the room. But that's not always the case.

Once I walked into the room of a patient and was met with wall-to-wall people packed in like sardines. Snack trays and beverages covered every available surface, and the television set was blasting a football game. I was fairly new and did that assuming thing as I took one of her sons aside. "Is this something she would want?" I questioned him.

"Oh, yes!" he quickly answered. "She was the queen of football parties. She lived to host huge gatherings like this every Sunday." My bad! That was a valuable lesson learned.

People usually mean well when trying to bring peace to their dying person, but again, it's sometimes difficult for them to know the right thing to do. I went to the home of my patient Paul one day and found him to have changed significantly since my visit a couple of days before. When I arrived, his wife and two adult daughters from a previous marriage were present at his bedside. As I began my assessment, I noticed changes that led me to think his time was running out. His breathing rate picked up tempo, and with each breath, his tongue began to thrust forward, just slightly past his lips.

"Oh," I told the women, "I think he's probably only got minutes left."

Each one of the women picked up a body part: one on each side grabbed a hand, and the last held his foot. They all began stroking their chosen piece of their loved one. "It's okay, you can go, Dad, it's okay," they said seemingly in unison. "We love you." I told them I would go into the kitchen to do some charting, and they could come and get me when they were ready. As I left, I continued to hear their chants telling him they loved him and he could go ahead and leave.

Twenty or thirty minutes later I was surprised they hadn't come to get me yet, so I went back in to check on them. He was still breathing and they were still chanting, "It's okay, Dad, you can go."

I studied Paul for a moment and then asked, "Is he the kind of guy that liked you doting on him?"

I looked up as one of the women dropped his hand and said, "I have to go to the bathroom." The other two women also dropped their body parts and followed suit, leaving me alone with Paul. I left after a minute and joined the women in the kitchen. I explained that sometimes we seem to have the ability to keep people here without meaning to, which took me all of three minutes. Then I returned to the room to find Paul had died.

Through the years, I've heard many hospice clinicians say it is important for the loved ones of our patients to tell them, "It's okay to go." My spin on that take is that it really isn't okay for someone you love to die. So I have a little different speech.

"You don't have to tell them it's okay," I would advise. "But you can say that *you* will be okay, because you will." In later years, I gained yet a different perspective, which was influenced by a couple of very seasoned hospice social workers: It isn't always okay to say okay. Saying it too often can set up a stressor if the patient isn't ready to leave. What most dying people seem to want to know is that those they cared about will be cared for and that their life had meaning and purpose. Also, if you're telling your loved one it will be okay but you don't really believe it, that won't convince the dying person to let go. If you think I'm implying that people have a choice of when they die, sometimes it seems they kind of do.

One of the most unbelievable things I ever saw was when I had a dying patient whose daughter seemingly brought her back to life. The family had called me into the room to tell me she had died. I placed my stethoscope on her chest and listened for one, then two full minutes. While I was doing this, the woman's youngest daughter was on the bed, bawling her eyes out and wailing, "Don't go, don't go."

Her siblings were telling her, "You have to let her go, you have to tell her it's okay."

So her cries changed to, "It's okay,"—sob—"it's okay." Clearly it was not okay, and I'll be damned if just as I was about to pronounce her time of death, my patient took a gasping breath! She lived for several more hours until finally the daughter had calmed down. And then she died. For real.

Acknowledging the truth about dying and its inevitability can make the difference between a terrible death experience and a beautiful one. This is more than just being present with our dying person in whatever way they need us to be; it's about fully embracing the experience, even if it isn't going the way we hoped.

Gladys was a sixty-nine-year-old with pancreatic cancer. My visits with her always included her husband, Stanley, and their daughter, Trina. Gladys was a fighter and had fought her disease so hard that her petite body was skeletal. It was hard to believe by looking at her that she could be in denial about her illness, but she was. Part of her fight included "working out" at her local gym. I say "working out" with quotation marks because when I became worried that she was putting herself at an increased risk for falls, I asked the occupational therapist to accompany her and evaluate her safety. The report back was that Gladys's workout was actually just her sitting on an exercise bike and visiting with the fellow gym rats she had known from twenty years of having gone there. As she grew weaker, I was finally able to get her to accept a hospice aide to assist her. The intent was to have the aide help her shower, but Gladys insisted that wasn't necessary. Instead, she asked her to wash the windows in the living room, where her hospital bed was, so she could see outside better. The aide complied without complaint. She understood that sometimes quality of life includes clean windows.

Gladys had a lot of pain from her cancer and wasn't very reliable about taking her bowel medications. As a result, she would often get constipated, which required me to administer a suppository. We would excuse ourselves to the bathroom from the kitchen table, where our visits took place, and Gladys would gingerly yank her size zero jeans down over her bony hips, revealing Victoria's Secret Pink panties. "My favorites too!" I told her the first time I saw them.

The family dynamic was interesting to say the least. They all bickered constantly, especially Stanley and Gladys with each other. But for some reason, it wasn't annoying to me. I could see through the petty arguments to the love this family had for one another and the unspoken grief at their impending loss. Unfortunately, as a hospice nurse, I am only minimally equipped to provide grief counseling, and although I offered multiple times to have my team social worker visit, they adamantly stated they only wanted me. What I realized, though, is they didn't want to try to have anyone "fix" what was happening in their relationships. That was their coping mechanism.

Gladys's decline was lingering, *very* lingering. The final weeks dragged on as she became thinner and thinner and spent more time sleeping than awake. Her pain had increased to where oral opioids were no longer effective, and I started an infusion. As we approached July, Trina started to voice concerns that her mom was going to die on her birthday, which would not only forever mar the date but also spoil her plans to go on a weeklong trip to eastern Washington. No judgment—I'll reiterate that people cope how they need to cope. As much as Gladys was deteriorating, Trina's birthday was still a little more than a week away, and I honestly couldn't see her living that much longer. Yet day after day she continued to breathe.

I was making daily visits to continue trying to manage Gladys's pain, which unfortunately wasn't going well, despite continued increases to the medication infusing into her implanted chest port. She wasn't in constant agony, but she complained of a nagging discomfort. Transferring to an inpatient setting was out of the question—she wanted to die in the house where she had raised her children and lived for the past forty years.

Every day Trina would lament her worries, which vacillated between "I hope she doesn't die on my birthday . . . I just know she's going to die on my birthday . . . She better not die on my birthday" and a more accepting stance, "She's probably going to die on my birthday, it would be just like her to do that!" It became the theme of Gladys's dying process. This family had endeared themselves to me with their joyful personalities and use of humor as a coping mechanism, so I knew this running joke was just much-needed comedic relief. Usually, it was just me and Stanley she would say these things to, but occasionally she would lean over to her now mostly unresponsive mom and utter something like, "Mom, I'm going to be so pissed if you ruin my birthday!"

By the time Trina's birthday was just days away, she had resigned herself to the fact that her mom very well could die on her birthday, and I started to get the feeling that as much as she seemed to dread the idea, she secretly hoped that sharing the day of her birth with the day of her mom's death would in some weird way validate the love they had for each other. On the day I got the call that Gladys had finally died, the date came as no surprise.

"Happy birthday," I said solemnly to Trina as she opened the door to let me in.

"It's not like I wasn't expecting it," she said with a chuckle. "You know how she was!" Although I had only known her for about four months, I did know "how she was"—someone who would not want anyone to easily forget her.

It might seem inconsiderate of Gladys to have died on her daughter's birthday. As it turned out, Trina viewed it as a cathartic experience, whether coincidence or contrived. It was a day they would always share. It's a good reminder: People die on birthdays. They die on Mother's Day, Father's Day, and all the other possible holidays and special occasions. I reiterate that death is not convenient. When people tell me that they have had a special day ruined forever because their person died on that day, I ask them to consider reframing how they view the occasion, just as Trina did.

So how does acknowledgment of our eventual demise change how we live? Well, for me, my life has been greatly influenced by the death of my patients. I think most people would find it impossible not to value the opportunity to continue living when you witness so many others who don't get that chance. But I don't think you have to be a hospice nurse to have your life impacted by the presence of death. We will all die someday, and acceptance of that fact gives us the freedom to live in a more fulfilled way. We can be rid of the fear in the back of our minds plaguing and overwhelming us, because there's only one way to not regret your own inevitable death: to live as fully as possible, in the moment, *right now.*

And I'm not going to lie; for some reason, coming to believe that there is an afterlife also helps me to worry less. To some, that may sound ironic, because if you believe there's no afterlife, that will make you want to live your life better, since you only get one crack at it. But for others, like me, if you think that in the end the lights go out and there's just nothing but dark, that might make you worry that the life you're living is meaningless. Like what is even the point if we don't get to keep our life experiences and memories?

I guess the moral of the story is most of us don't want to feel like our time on Earth wasn't well spent. Whether there's an afterlife or not, I hope my legacy is the lesson that letting go of your fear of death can help you to embrace each day with grace and gratitude—and convince you to have a fucking blast while you have the chance.

EPILOGUE

My ability to be a successful DeathTok influencer culminated from years of experience in death care. At the time I started my TikTok platform, I had been working in hospice for sixteen years. While most of my work as a hospice nurse was doing direct patient care, I had been ready for a break when I accepted the quality position. It didn't have anything to do with the emotional stress of being with dying people—for me, there wasn't any; I loved being a guide on such an important journey for my patients and their families. The truth is I was sick of Seattle's traffic-ridden nightmare commute. Life is too damn short to waste any of it sitting in a freeway parking lot. My new position enabled me to work most of the time from home and still help hospice patients by improving the quality of care provided by the other nurses still there in person.

As satisfied as I am with my current role in hospice quality, which enables me to work virtually, I do sometimes miss providing direct patient care. However, through my social media, I have been given a gift to continue helping so many people who are experiencing or have experienced their own struggles around death, be it the loss of their loved one, their own approaching death, or even just death anxiety.

Being a social media influencer is not without challenges, no matter what you're influencing about. There are people who seem to get up in the morning, get on social media, scroll through videos, and leave nasty comments like it's their job. Being a death influencer adds to the challenge because there are people who think that hospice nurses are in it just to cause their patients to die faster. There is actually a whole Facebook group dedicated to telling stories of how hospice murdered their loved ones!

I'd be lying if I said the cruelty *never* got under my skin. But for the most part I usually chalk up hateful comments to displaced grief and ignore them. Life is also too short to give a shit about what other people think about me—something I wish I would've known when I was a teenager facing all those bullies.

Knowing that there are more people who appreciate and value the education and information that I am providing than there are trolls makes dealing with the hate easier. I have received countless comments, messages, and emails from people telling me that they have learned so much from my videos, that they have a better understanding and acceptance of their mortality, that their death anxiety has significantly improved or disappeared, or that the guilt they felt over their person's death and how things went is resolved. All of that is validation that I am making an important difference in people's lives.

The onset of the COVID-19 pandemic didn't just propel me into social media influencing, it also facilitated a major life change for me and Randy. My hospice position became completely virtual, and after a month of sheltering in place at our cabin on a mountain in eastern Washington, we made a few big decisions: Randy retired early, and we sold our home, packed up our cat, Pam, and moved to the cabin permanently. Leaving our home in the city was a little sad, but not because of the conveniences we were giving up. Being a gardening fanatic, I had accumulated many flowers from my patients and some amazing peonies my dad had given me, which I had to leave behind. We didn't have any area to replant them that would be safe from the deer that roamed our mountainous yard. I was willing to make the sacrifice.

We'd originally purchased our ten-acre lot as a vacation getaway. Our property is bordered to the north by national forest and to the west by state land, which provides nearly infinite privacy and seclusion. We had a local contractor work from plans Randy designed to build the shell of the cabin, and we spent our first vacations there finishing it. If someone had told me in my clubbing days that I would someday be willingly living in a cabin in the woods with no power, no running water, and an outhouse, I *never* would have believed it. I sometimes think if it wasn't for social media, which thankfully I can access through a satellite dish, I wouldn't be able to survive such a clandestine life! But being able to stay connected to other humans while living in a literal paradise is unbeatable.

You might be wondering, but what about the alcoholism? Didn't that impact your parenting, your life, your schooling, your career? Surprisingly, no. Although I definitely had bouts of being drunk beyond belief, I was very much a functional alcoholic for many years. And I never did go back to doing drugs again, other than occasionally smoking pot.

It wasn't until Randy and I got together that the alcoholic in me started to resurface in a much more problematic way. Partying was what brought us together. We loved drinking and had fun doing it with each other. The problems it caused at first weren't significant, mostly bad hangovers for me and sometimes little arguments between us. As time went on, we recognized that it was an issue, and we tried everything you can imagine to manage our drinking so we wouldn't have to resort to quitting altogether—only drinking on the weekends, only drinking beer or wine, trying an app for moderating, going to AA and Smart Recovery. I even bought a breathalyzer to track our blood alcohol content. That didn't help, because I couldn't even wait the twenty minutes between drinks required for an accurate reading!

Nothing worked, and the only saving grace for either of us not frying our livers was that in the last nine years of our marriage, he worked nights and I worked days, so the only time we drank was on the weekends. Well, on the weekends and anytime we went to the cabin, which presented us with another complication. If we were going to retire in our cabin, we had to quit drinking. The association of partying with being there was going to be too prevalent to overcome. Good health is vital to living an off-grid, homesteading lifestyle—also, booze is expensive! We had to commit to sobriety once and for all.

For Randy, that meant going up to the cabin by himself for three weeks to get ready for the move without any temptation. For me, it was making an announcement on TikTok. As I learned with my website getting me through nursing school, accountability is motivating. Having awareness that over a hundred thousand social media followers would be watching my sober journey was *very* motivating! Both of our plans worked, and together, we've now shared more than four years of sobriety.

Shortly after Randy and I moved to our mountain, Wayne, a man in his late sixties, bought a twenty-acre parcel next to us. His wife had recently died, and he decided that he wanted to fulfill his dream of mountain life despite the fact that he had a heart condition. Over the course of a couple of years, he began moving his belongings up to his property, including a trailer, and he would often come up and camp. Then he suddenly died from a heart attack. His family agreed to sell us the property, and when I met with them to sign the documents, they expressed sadness that he hadn't been able to make his dream a reality. "I disagree," I told them. "Even though Wayne was never able to live here full time, he was living his dream.

He bought the property, he spent a lot of time here, and he was moving onto it."

Death is sad, death is scary, but mostly, death is an inconvenience. No matter what kind of a planner you are, death never seems to come at a good time. Don't wait to fulfill your dreams until you know that you're going to be able to complete them, because that day may never come. Ever heard the saying "Life is short and then you die"? There are no truer words, and for some, life is very short.

Our views on life can influence how we die. More importantly, our views on death can influence how we live, and in the end that is what really matters. Death is just a moment at the end of our journey, while life is hopefully more long-lasting. The ultimate truth about life and death is that one does not exist without the other. Over my life, I've had many views on dying, from wishing for it, to fearing it, to finally accepting the inevitability of it. It was the acceptance that has had the most meaningful impact on how I live. I know now that whatever time we get to live is truly a gift that should never be taken for granted. As the old saying goes, life is not about the destination; it's about the journey. Mine has been one helluva ride, and there's more to come. Until I die. Which I will, because we all do in the end—and I accept that. You should too.

ACKNOWLEDGMENTS

Where do I begin? There are so many people who have shaped my life to where I felt like I had something of value to offer the universe.

If you've made it this far, you know by now that I am far from religious, yet I have no problem saying I have truly been blessed with the most amazing offspring ever. Reader, if you have more than one child, you will understand this caveat: I put this in order of age . . . not favorite!

Keith, thank you for forgiving the sins of the mother, for being kind and caring to everyone, an amazing dad to my grandpeeps, and for using your IT degree to fix Mom's computer.

Eden, my "little cone" (there's an inside joke there, obvi), this book would not have been completed without you. I will always cherish the memory of us lying in bed together at the Airbnbs in Anaheim and New Jersey, reading through the chapters, wordsmithing, writing, and rewriting. You're a fantastic social worker, but if you ever decide to change careers, you would be an awesome editor.

Mia, my mini-me, who made it into LAW SCHOOL! Thank you for your unwavering support. You always give me credit for the amazing woman you have become, but the credit really needs to go to you for your perseverance and dedication to your endeavors.

To the rest of my family . . .

Randy, for being the most hilarious, hardest working, and most devoted husband with the best sawmill EVER.

Laura, my fav sister and twin soul. When you told me my book was a "page-turner," I don't think I've ever felt more proud. Of course, when you later walked that back a little by saying you thought that because you are a part of a lot of the story, I felt a smidge deflated. But what else are siblings for if not to keep egos checked and balanced! Still, you complete me in ways no one else can.

My brother, Brad, you've rescued me so many times in so many ways. I lucked out in the baby brother department with you.

Kaede-bug, you are always in my heart and on my mind. I wish for you the best life has to offer.

And to my parents, who tough-loved me enough to help set me on the right track.

Webbie, my BFF. You are hands down the nicest person I've ever known. I will never stop being amazed by how you stood by my side without judgment even when you were knee-deep in the crap I created. What was wrong with you? Just kidding. I couldn't have asked for a better ride-or-die.

Lisa and Halley, my hospice social worker friends and informal editors, thank you for believing in me and letting me know my story is important and needs to be shared.

Maggie, having you as a mentor was a gift that has never stopped giving throughout my hospice career. You are the reason I strived to become not just a good hospice nurse but a great one.

The sergeant at the police station, I'm sure I will never see you again, but I do hope if by chance you read this book, you will know how ultimately life-changing your words were.

To my social media followers, who give me a platform to educate about the one thing I've been most passionate about—normalizing death—I started influencing to make a difference in your life. In the end, it was you all who made a difference in mine.

To my publishing team at Girl Friday Productions . . . thank you!

And to pretty much every other person in my life whether you helped me or hurt me, because without you I wouldn't be who I am or where I am today. Thank you for being part of my journey.

Most importantly, to my patients and their families, for allowing me to participate in this most intimate and sacred time of your lives. It was an honor and a privilege. *Thank you.*

RESOURCES

Although this book has some educational components, it is a memoir, so is not exhaustive of all there is to know about death, dying, and hospice. Thus I wanted to include some recommendations for other informational material:

BOOKS

- *Hope for the Best, Plan for the Rest: 7 Keys for Navigating a Life-Changing Diagnosis* by Dr. Sammy Winemaker and Dr. Hsien Seow
- *Nothing to Fear: Demystifying Death to Live More Fully* by Julie McFadden, RN
- *Gone from my Sight: The Dying Experience* by Barbara Karnes, RN (and all other books she's written)
- *Hard Choices for Loving People: CPR, Feeding Tubes, Palliative Care, Comfort Measures, and the Patient with a Serious Illness, 6th Ed.* by Hank Dunn

WEBSITES

- **CaringInfo.org** Helps with informed decisions about hospice care before a crisis.
- **Endwellproject.org** A nonprofit organization striving to improve end-of-life care for all.
- **Medicare.gov/care-compare** Helps you select a hospice that's right for you.
- **Compassionandchoices.org** Information and resources for improving healthcare equity and empowering anyone on their end-of-life journey.
- **Giveamile.org** Provides free flights for people to travel to be with their loved ones on hospice.
- **Deathwithdignity.org** Information, resources, and advocacy for medical aid in dying in the United States.

ABOUT THE AUTHOR

Penny Hawkins Smith is a nationally certified hospice nurse with twenty years of experience. She has cared for thousands of dying people and is a passionate advocate for high-quality end-of-life care. Over two million people follow her on social media, where she uses storytelling, dark humor, and dance trends to normalize death and the dying process. She also shares her own inspirational stories of overcoming a tumultuous past.

Penny lives in Washington State with her husband, along with her cattle dog, Kevin, and Pam the cat. She works virtually as a hospice quality nurse from her off-the-grid cabin on a mountain, with a retirement plan in the works.

Facebook post, December 20, 2010

As I sit at the bedside holding the hand of my
dying patient until her family arrives, I can't
help but think I have the best job in the world.
What a privilege.